Jacki's story evokes ___ and unbelievably tangible. There is an undeniable portrayal ___ God's presence in her life. The level of love that she gives to others is a clear reflection of God's plan for her. Jacki is a walking miracle and her story will inevitably magnify the message of faith in God to a doubting world. I am greatly impacted by having Jacki in my life and consider it an honor to call her friend.

—AMEA A. ISOM
Executive Director, The Perfect Choice, Avondale, AZ

I encourage every believer who has ever struggled with any season of trials or sickness to read *Cancer With Grace*. It is a heartfelt, down to Earth account of God's grace in action through difficult times that challenge our faith in ways we don't always understand, strengthens our faith, and births a testimony of His goodness in the mist of our dark night. It is a personal account of God's great faithfulness that reveals the oftentimes hidden truth that "His grace is sufficient." This story is also a testimony of a strong family that faced and fought the giant cancer together and was victorious both physically and spiritually.

I have had the privilege of knowing Jacki and Barney and watching them walk through this difficult season with dignity and strong faith. I have been both amazed and encouraged at the manner and grace displayed during Jacki's battle with cancer. As her story unfolded, I found myself challenged and emboldened in my own faith as she, through the ups and downs and high and low seasons, found hope and strength even in small victories and unlikely people.

—DR. TONY WILLIAMS
Senior Pastor, Maranatha Christian Center, San Jose, CA

This story was ordained and destined to be told. As one privileged to be a dear longtime friend, I had a front row seat to watch the incredible transformation of this woman. When I met her, she was a newlywed moving to a new area and out of her comfort zone, a bit closed and guarded. Time and life has granted her wisdom and a great big heart, willing to babysit this single mom's children (and a bunch of others) for a few bucks and love them like her own. This book is just another one of the ways she has found to minister the Gospel. From wise words with a cup of coffee on her comfy couch to standing behind a podium to preach, she is the epitome of true ministry. I am certain God felt comfortable handing Jacki these difficult times because she had done the work to prove herself worthy and strong. God could count on her and trust her to turn this period of dry difficult times into a story of triumph and victory. Now, you are fortunate enough to get a glimpse into this wonderful life and testimony. I know you will enjoy it.

—ALICIA HARRIS
Technical Writer / Document Specialist, CH2M, Prudhoe Bay, AK

My friend, the imperishable Jac Jac, has created a legacy that every woman who faces an impossible situation should read and then customize for herself. Her purpose is intact; love and trust our praiseworthy Abba Father, then in spite of it all, dare to live fully and well. I am another Surviving Thriver, a graduate of the Global Women Leadership Network and International Certified Addiction Counselor ICADC—all after my own cancer journey, largely due to Jacki's example to dare to walk out her healing.

She dares, I dare. Be inspired by her testimony and you'll dare, too!

—LYNDA K. HALIBURTON
International Certified Addiction Counselor (ICAC),
CityTeam Ministries, San Jose, CA

As I read *Cancer With Grace,* I could not help but be totally swept away by the awesomeness of God. I cried, I laughed, and I praised the Lord as I read it! I went through my own journey of a diagnosis of cancer and totally identified with everything Jacki shared and today I know God as my healer, my provider and deliverer. I was diagnosed shortly after Jacki, but even as she was still going through her treatments she never stopped calling me to make sure I kept the faith!

Nobody can tell Jacki's testimony like she can! I love hearing it over and over! This is a book that I will share with others and definitely will read over and over again. God was right, This was not about Jacki or me! To God be the glory!

—COLLEEN HUDGEN
Executive Director, Live Oak Adult Day Care Services,
San Jose, CA

If I were given an opportunity to talk with the authors of the Webster's Dictionary to suggest a rewrite for the word "grace," I would recommend they simply use a picture of Jacquelyn D. Murray. *Cancer With Grace* is a demonstration of a girl next door that just happens to be every woman's hero. Jacki epitomizes the essence of a Christian woman that not only leads by example, but lives the example! *Cancer With Grace* will change your perspective on complaining.

—LA'TRESA M. JESTER
Overseer and Senior Pastor, Gideon Baptist Church, Tucson, AZ

Cancer With Grace grabs your heart! As I read, I felt as if I was sitting across the table from Jacki having a cup of coffee while she shared her journey through the train wrecks of emotion to the throne room of God's grace.

DENNIS WATSON
Associate Pastor, The Oasis Church, Tucson, AZ

CANCER

With

Grace

Trusting a God of
His word in trial

Jacquelyn D. Murray

Adam Colwell's
writeworks

Cancer With Grace
by Jacquelyn D. Murray

All Bible quotations, unless otherwise indicated, are from New International Version, Copyright © 1973, 1978, 1984, 2011 by Biblica, Inc. Used by permission. All rights reserved worldwide.

Adam Colwell's WriteWorks Publishing
Adam Colwell's WriteWorks LLC, Tucson, AZ
Copyright © 2015 by Jacquelyn D. Murray

All rights reserved. Published 2015
Printed in the United States of America

Edited by Adam Colwell
Cover design by Barney Hilton Murray
Interior design and typesetting by Katherine Lloyd, The DESK
Interior floral art by Alisa Foytik/BigStock
Printing by BookLogix, Alpharetta, GA

ISBN 978-0-9892057-7-1

Dedication

This book is dedicated to my Lord and Savior Jesus Christ. I am so grateful for all you have done for me, in me, and through me. You have loved me unconditionally. You have saved me from a life of sin. You have been faithful. Thank you for being by my side throughout this process. Without you, I never would have made it.

Acknowledgements

Barney—My husband *and* my boyfriend! Thank you for being the man of God that will step up to the plate every time. You were the little boy standing next to my high chair at my first birthday party. Who would have known that you would be the man who would stand by my side fifty years later as I went through one of the hardest times in my life? Thank you for holding me up physically, emotionally, and spiritually when I couldn't hold myself up. You were and always will be my strength. Thank you for the prayers that kept me on the right side of crazy. Thank you for loving me even when I was unlovable. I love you so very much.

Aja Canai—I'm so proud of the woman, wife, and mother you've become! You're stronger than you know and wise beyond your years. Thank you for being there for me in so many ways throughout this journey. I love you.

Aryn DeLano—What can I say? You've endured more in your young life than I could ever imagine. And you have done it with grace, courage, and strength. I admire you and I'm so proud of you. You're a wonderful woman and mother. Your tenacity encouraged me to walk tall through this journey. Thank you for all you do! I love you.

Glenn and Delawn—Thank you for helping my daughters as they watched their mom go through such a serious illness. I know it was hard for them and both of you. I appreciate all that you've both done for them and for me. My prayer is that you were able to see God in my life as I walked the walk.

Aren Kai and Arilàn DeLano—My first set of grands! Every day you bring joy and laughter to my life! I am thankful to God for allowing me the opportunity to share in your lives on a regular basis. You kept a smile in my heart through all of this. My constant prayer was to be able to watch you grow. God is answering that prayer!

Alijah Kindred and Ajani Wynell—My second set of grands! Thank you for being my encouragement to live. My prayer to the Lord was that I would be able to see you two come into the world…and that I would be well enough to enjoy you both. You were my inspiration. He is a good God!

Lauren—A very special grandchild not by birth, but in my heart. Thanks for just being you!

Asè Kaamil and Aizak Hilton Kole—I didn't know you would become part of my life. But I'm so glad the Lord spared my life to see you!

Mommy—No matter how old your children are, they will always be your "little girl" or "little boy." I can't begin to imagine how difficult it was for you to go through another child's illness. Thank you for being the praying woman that you are. Your steadfastness with the Lord taught me the lessons I needed for this time. Your strength through your own illness was a reminder of God's healing power. I love you.

Gene and Daryl—My "little" brothers. Watching your big sis go through such a serious illness could not have been easy, especially after losing a sibling just a couple of years earlier. Thank you for your prayers, calls, and support. They really meant a lot to me. You guys rock!

Lori—Baby sis…thank you for *always* being there. The sacrifice of your time, finances, and energy mean a lot. You're a woman of few words which, of course, you can't help in this family. But you know the old saying, "Actions speak louder than words." You've shown over and over again how loyal and caring you are to me. I'm grateful to the Lord for you and I'll always remember your kindness.

Lisa—As a person, I think you're pretty cool. As a friend, I think you're amazing. As *my* friend, I think you're the best! Thank you for giving me the title of this book and your prayers, support and encouragement. I love you with every bit of my blood pressure damaged-artery clogged by ham hocks and bacon-but still pumping pretty good-heart!

Adam Colwell—My editor, publisher, mentor, and new friend. Thank you for the many weeks of mentoring and teaching. The time we spent together was invaluable. Most of all, thank you for allowing me to be me and taking those hours of taped interviews and helping me to bring them to life on paper. You're an amazing editor and an even better man of God. I could not have finished this without you, my friend!

All of my special friends—"Thank you" just doesn't seem adequate for what I feel in my heart. There are so many of you that are so important to me. I can't begin to name all of you. Surely, I would forget someone. Nor could I list all of the things you've done, not just during the time of my illness, but in general. Please know that I cherish each one of you and thank you from the bottom of my heart. My prayer is that the Lord will bless you in all that you do!

Chapter One

"Okay—now what's going on?"

I said it aloud, and I thought my husband Barney might've heard me, though I couldn't be sure. The loud pop in my right ear that had prompted my reactionary question also instantly took away my ability to hear out of that ear. It was as if it was suddenly flooded with water, blocking out the triumphant tunes reverberating around me. We were in church, right in the middle of Sunday morning worship service. I tried to keep singing, but I could barely make out my own voice, much less the chorus.

I let out a heavy sigh. There were few things I enjoyed doing more than singing praise to my God.

I could've shown more frustration, I suppose. The sudden hearing loss was just the latest of a quintet of health problems to invade my life's path over the past five months—but I didn't want to burden anyone else with my issues. I was the go-to girl for others. Mother, wife, daughter, friend, leader, mentor—I was always somebody for someone else, and these were roles I treasured. I'm the one that should have all the answers, not the problems. The administrator in me served to keep things orderly and in perspective. Besides, I never saw myself as overly emotional.

It started in January, when my doctor told me I had diabetes. As a middle-aged black woman who didn't drink, smoke or do drugs, I enjoyed my culinary pleasures of rice, pasta, and soda, so that diagnosis wasn't surprising. It was discouraging, though, since the main reason we moved to the desert was so we could be here to help our daughters Aja and Aryn care for our grand-children. Getting sick was not part of the plan.

Then, the same week I was scheduled to return to my doctor to follow-up on the start of my diabetes treatments, I acquired a persistent earache in my right ear. My doctor took a look and said she thought it was an infection, so she prescribed antibiotics and the pain subsided. As soon as the medicine ran out, though, the earache returned and brought along a companion, a headache. While the doctor tried other solutions that ended up being inef-fective, the headaches progressed to where it even hurt to lay my head on my pillow at night. A few weeks later, I awoke one morning and could barely open my mouth wide enough to brush my teeth. Lockjaw was diagnosed, an added nuisance since it loosened during the day but tightened up again each night. The pain from everything worsened and became constant. I popped ibuprofen tablets like they were M&Ms.

I had another, far better constant through all of this. Barney was even-keeled and consistent, my rock of stability and the perfect balance for my personality. I often jerked awake in pain, crying in the middle of the night. Barney was always ready with a comforting word or prayer of faith, and I drew strength from him. This was not without its hazards for my husband. There was one night he prayed for me and, without knowing it, laid his hand on the very side of my head that was splitting with pain. "Barney," I stated firmly, "please—take—your—hand—off—of—my—head." He instantly complied. It was a good thing. I was about to send him flying onto the floor.

> Barney was even-keeled and consistent, my rock of stability.

By July, the time came to drive to California for two events I was much anticipating: a meeting of the Daughters of Zion, a non-profit group for which I served on the board of directors; and the twentieth-anniversary celebration of Maranatha Christian Center, our longtime home church. Barney and I were dealing with more stress by then: he'd lost his job in June, meaning we were at that moment without health insurance. I hadn't been to the doctor in weeks. My head was banging so badly I slept for most of the twelve-hour drive to San Jose, but I was feeling slightly better for the Daughters of Zion meeting on Friday. We planned our upcoming conference and visited with our keynote speaker who had flown in from North Carolina. When we shared prayer requests at the close of the day, I finally told someone other than Barney and my family what was going on with my health, from the diabetes diagnosis all the way through to the lockjaw.

The lady from North Carolina spoke up. "I know a woman who had symptoms just like yours."

Hope leaped in my heart. "Really?" I asked. "What happened to her?"

"She died."

She didn't divulge what she died from, and I certainly didn't ask. The group entered into prayer and my need was mentioned, but I don't remember a word that was spoken. All I could think was *"She died."*

I was in my usual haze of pain on Saturday, but I didn't tell Barney what the woman had said. He had enough to worry about as it was. Late that morning, we went to the rehearsal for the Sunday celebration service. I was asked to sing on the platform as part of the worship team, and I didn't want to refuse, despite having lost half of my hearing. The next day, there's no telling how off-key I sounded, though there must've been a problem, because the woman standing next to me kept leaning close so I could hear the words and notes better. Unfortunately, she was on my right side, so I heard nary a note.

I didn't tell anyone in the worship team or at the church what was going on, either. I just didn't want to get into it. I didn't even know what to say. I had no idea what was really going on.

In September, Barney got a contract position working for our son-in-law Glenn at IBM, allowing him to get limited health insurance benefits. At the advice of my doctor, I immediately called to make an appointment with an ear, nose, and throat specialist named Dr. Joe Huerta. I couldn't be seen until Monday, October 22. That day, I went by myself to see the specialist since Barney was at work. After the initial examination, though Dr. Huerta didn't express any specific concern, he confirmed the hearing loss and referred me for a CT scan. On Friday of that same week, I woke up to find the right side of my face swollen up like a puffy cushion, and the pain was intense. I called Dr. Huerta's office and was told to come right in.

"Did you get the CT scan yet?" he asked as he attempted to open my mouth wide enough to take a closer look inside. It hurt like crazy.

"No, they still haven't called me back," I responded as I held back tears from the pain.

"We're going to get you in for that on Monday. Until then, I'm going to get you Percocet for the weekend. It should hold you over."

Early Monday morning, I went in for the CT scan. As I was prepped for the scan, the technician explained that it would be for the right side of my neck.

What to do when you don't know what to do

"For I know the plans I have for you," declares the Lord, "plans to prosper you and not to harm you, plans to give you hope and a future." —Jeremiah 29:11

There will be times in our lives when we find ourselves in a quandary—perplexed, uncertain, in a dilemma, when we ask ourselves and God, "What in the world is going on?" Finding out I had a rare head and neck cancer put me in that position. In this passage from Jeremiah, the prophet is sending a letter to the captives in Babylon with a message from God. First, he let them know that everything wasn't going to be peaches and cream. They would be in exile for seventy years! But he follows that news with God's promise of hope and prosperity for their future.

We can be assured that God has a plan for our future. He knows what's ahead and His purposes for us are always good and positive. We must believe this—even when going through the painful situations in our lives. Life cannot and *will not* stand still just because we endure trouble. Trial is temporary and we always have God to help us through.

What is it that you are facing in your life that has left you not knowing what to do? Trust that God knows all about it and that He has a plan for you. Push through to receive His promise.

"No," I said. "That must be a mistake. It's my ear."

He looked at his papers. "I'm sorry, Mrs. Murray, but your doctor said this is definitely for your neck."

I was confused but also didn't want to argue, so into the CT tube I went. I was back home by 10:00 a.m. Minutes later I received a call from Dr. Huerta. "I don't like what I see," he said. "I want you to go to the hospital at two o'clock and have a biopsy."

"This afternoon?" I asked. *That's fast. A biopsy. Do I have a tumor?*

Aja drove me to the hospital and Barney arrived at the hospital from work shortly after I arrived. As the pathologist was getting me ready, he told me he was going to take the biopsy sample from my neck, and I again disagreed, insisting the problem was with my ear. "No," he corrected, "you have a lump in your neck." That was the first time the word "lump" was used by anyone, and he asked if I wanted to feel it. He led my hand to the spot and, sure enough, there it was. It was about the size of a piece of Good and Plenty candy, but not as hard. In fact, it was a bit mushy to the touch and, surprisingly, didn't hurt at all. As he manipulated my neck muscles to let me feel the lump, I watched as Barney slowly slid down the side of the wall next to me. He had fainted. This alarmed me more than the biopsy. Whatever was going on with me, I knew I was going to need Barney's strength to carry me through. He couldn't be sick, too! A nurse came in, revived him, and moved him to a chair. The pathologist then prepped the needle and asked if I wanted to numb the area; I told him I'd be okay without it. The needle went in. Aja was there but stayed out of sight behind the curtain. It was all too much for her.

First sample taken, the pathologist returned moments later.

"I need to get another sample," he said. "I do see some

abnormally shaped cells, but we need to run more tests. I'll make sure the doctor calls you as soon as we know more." With that, I decided to accept the anesthesia this time around, and he took the second sample of cells. We went on our way, and that evening my thoughts were generally upbeat. I assumed it could be cancer, but I

> "I don't want to talk on the phone," he said. "It's serious."

figured if it was, they'd just go in and cut it out. Simple.

It wasn't until late the next morning that I heard back from Dr. Huerta.

"I don't want to talk on the phone," he said. "It's serious. I need to see you right away. Don't get an appointment. Just come in."

I glanced at the clock on the wall, not because I needed to know what time it was, but just to give my eyes something to do. "Should I bring my husband with me?" I asked, already knowing the answer.

"By all means."

Barney came from work in his car and met me at Dr. Huerta's office. We were quickly ushered back to a standard issue exam room with a bed, chair, charts and art prints on the wall. This artificially homey atmosphere was diminished by the medical equipment and the harsh glow of the florescent lights. Dr. Huerta entered the room, then hesitated, shuffling his feet. He seemed more nervous than I was.

His expression wasn't stern, but it was solemn. "You have Squamous Cell Carcinoma of the Nasopharynx."

I tried to process the jargon, but I had no idea what the nasopharynx was, much less anything else. "What does all that mean?"

"You have three malignant tumors in your nasal cavity." He

pointed to one of the wall charts and showed where the naso-pharynx was located.

"So you mean I have cancer?"

"Yes."

"Okay," I said, monotone, as though I were a three-year-old responding to being gently scolded for not brushing my teeth. "How soon before I can have surgery?"

"Surgery is not an option," Dr. Huerta said. "The tumors have been growing too long. One of them is too big, and in too sensitive an area to have surgery. You'll need to have chemotherapy and radiation."

So much for my "cut it out quick" theory. "Are you kidding me?" I said, not in an accusing manner, but in a way that suggested I didn't think the doctor was serious—though in reality I heard him loud and clear. Barney remained characteristically silent. Moments later, we went out to sit in the waiting room while Dr. Huerta's assistant called an oncologist. I realized I wasn't acting like someone who had just been told they had cancer. In a way, it was a relief. After ten months of having all of these things happen to me without knowing why, at least now I knew what it was. Still, there was no screaming, no dramatic breakdown, not even a tear. At that moment, I simply wasn't alarmed. My attitude was, *Whatever has to be done, let's just do it.* The assistant put me on the phone with the specialist. My appointment was set for Thursday, two days later.

As we left Dr. Huerta's office, Barney and I decided we'd drive in our separate vehicles to see Aja and her husband Glenn. On the way there, I'd call Aryn in Phoenix and tell her the news. I started driving, but before I picked up my phone, I sensed the voice of God. He was speaking to my spirit in His concise, unmistakable way—like His voice and no other.

"This isn't about you, Jacki," the Lord said. "This is about the testimony that is going to come out of it. I will get the glory." With His word, I had a peace that somehow, someway, everything ultimately was going to be okay—even though I didn't know yet if "okay" meant my healing would happen in this life or the next. I also had no idea what chemotherapy and radiation was going to be like.

I then called Aryn. She's always been the less emotional of my two girls, and her response reflected that. I could tell she was taken aback, but because she studied biology and chemistry in college, she was as much fascinated as frightened. "Wow, Mom," she concluded. "This is going to be hard, but I know you can do it!" Not knowing what I was in for, her faith encouraged me. We were saying our goodbyes as I pulled in next to Barney's car outside of Aja's house. I knew I had to be careful with Aja. I had to break this to her in just the right way, or she was going to fall apart. The last thing I wanted was for anyone to lose it.

Barney and I took a seat on the family room couch, and Glenn leaned over the couch behind us. Aja and baby Aren sat on the floor in front of us. I told her the diagnosis matter-of-factly, like I was giving tomorrow's weather forecast. "Don't worry," I added. "We've already talked to the oncologist and have an appointment on Thursday." But my attempt at calm was falling short. Aja was starting to shake and her eyes were welling up.

Glenn jumped in: "And Jacki, don't you worry, either. We've already been looking for day care for the baby. You won't have to take care of Aren as you go through all of this."

I lost it.

By "lost" it, I mean total mega meltdown. It wasn't pretty.

"Please don't take him from me," I wailed, weeping. "It'll help me to have Aren. I promise if I can't do it, I'll let you know. Just

How to hear and respond to the voice of God

My sheep listen to my voice; I know them,
and they follow me. —John 10:27

When I was pregnant with our first child, it amazed me the way she responded to the sound of her father's voice. It represented the one who would teach and guide her through life, and love, cherish, and protect her. By the time she was born, his voice had become familiar to her. He is her father.

Similarly, the children of God are familiar with His voice. We are His sheep and He offers the same love and protection to us. In John 10, the Jewish leaders tried to trip up Jesus by questioning whether He was indeed the Messiah. His answer here was simple but profoundly direct. He was telling them, "If *you* knew me, you would recognize my voice."

You can become familiar with the voice of God by spending time with Him in prayer, studying His Word, and fellowshipping with the Spirit. Over the years, that trio has allowed me to become familiar with His voice. I knew I had to follow and believe what He was saying during my journey with cancer. That kind of faith only comes from a place of assurance in knowing your Shepherd.

Learn to spend some quality time with your Good Shepherd. Know His voice—then follow what He says.

don't take my baby away!" Then I sank into what Barney calls "the ugly cry." I was too lost in my suffering to know how Aja was responding.

Sometime in the next few minutes, Barney asked Glenn if he could work half days from home. That way he could get me back and forth to treatments and help me take care of Aren, who we only had for a few hours each day as it was. Glenn agreed, and I slowly pulled myself back together. We left after an hour or so and made the brief drive home.

Once home, my inner administrator took charge. I called all my immediate relatives while Barney contacted his. They were all on the East Coast and it was getting late at night there, so we knew we had to hurry. Barney had fewer calls and finished way before I did. In the interest of time, I went into as little detail as I could with most of the family, and did not allow anyone to pray for me. That offended a few of them, and I understand that; prayer was likely the one thing they felt they could do to help at that moment. I also knew, though, that I'd have another breakdown if the prayers got too deep and too real, and I simply didn't want to experience that ugly cry again tonight. I wrapped up the final call just short of ten o'clock. Barney and I then settled in to our usual nightly routine and in short order went straight to bed. Neither one of us said another word about cancer—or anything else.

The next day was just as routine—until Barney got home from work.

"So, we have company coming," he said.

"We what?"

"Didn't you get a call from Bill?" he asked.

"Nope."

He revealed that Bill, a longtime friend from Sacramento, had contacted him at work and said his wife Gloria was already on her way to go with us to the oncologist tomorrow. She wanted to help by being there to take notes, ask needed questions, and so on. She arrived a few hours later and stayed the night with us. I'm so glad she came. The next day, she joined me, Barney, and baby Aren in the waiting room of Dr. Steven Ketchel, my chemotherapy oncologist. It still didn't seem real to me, yet God made His presence clear when an older couple came in and sat near us. After a few minutes, the husband was called to the back, and his wife was visibly upset.

"Are you okay?" I asked her.

She looked up at me and attempted a smile. "I'm just so worried about my husband."

Without a second thought, we gathered around her, held hands, and offered up a prayer for her and her husband. I felt so much compassion for the woman that I forgot, if just for that fleeting moment, that I was actually there as a patient, too. Yet I already knew I had plenty of people praying for me, and I loved being able to pray for her.

Moments later, it was my turn to be called. Dr. Ketchel spoke in mind-numbing detail about how I was first going to have chemotherapy to shrink the tumor. He said it would be an "aggressive" treatment that started with him but then continued at home as I gave myself treatments with a special pump that required me to have a catheter. He explained that the radiation treatments that followed would cause sores in my mouth, so I would need outpatient surgery to place a feeding tube in addition to the catheter. He spoke of chemicals and medicines and said the treatment period should last about four months.

> I already knew I had plenty of people praying for me.

My mind was reeling. Gloria and her notes were a Godsend.

However, she had to return to California the next day, Friday, before I met with Dr. Michael Manning, my radiation oncologist. Barney joined me for that appointment, and I spent the first forty-five minutes talking to a resident as he interviewed me about my medical history. He also revealed how ridiculously rare my cancer was: only one percent of Americans get it. In fact, he said it's most prevalent in Asian men who are heavy smokers—and here I was, an African-American woman who'd never lifted a cigarette to her lips since high school.

Dr. Manning arrived. He said the tumor had started in my nasal cavity and then spread into my neck. It was large and had advanced to a Stage Four cancer. It was to be taken quite seriously. He listed more details: I'd need another scan to see if the cancer had spread anywhere else in my body; a stomach tube would have to be surgically inserted for supplemental feeding during radiation; the treatments would be twice per day, five days per week, for six weeks; possible side effects would be sores in the mouth and throat, problems swallowing and tasting, dry skin, and extreme fatigue. Plus, since the radiation was going to be administered to my head, any necessary dental work should be done as soon as possible. As it turned out, that meant no less than five new crowns. I should've told the dentist to just take all my teeth and give me dentures.

Dr. Manning finished his discourse, and I took it all in. He was less friendly than Dr. Ketchel—not mean, but also not nearly as personable.

"When we finish," I asked, "is that going to get all of the cancer?"

He shook his head. "I don't think so."

Not exactly what I wanted to hear. "Okay. Will it get ninety percent?"

"I don't think so."

How to endure suffering

For it is commendable if someone bears up under the pain of unjust suffering because they are conscious of God. —1 Peter 2:19

*L*et's face it. We all have hardship, fear, and painful suffering in our lives. That's just part of life. But we're not always willing to embrace those difficulties. Who *wants* to suffer? I could have thought of so many more ways to bring glory to God than going through cancer! But I learned through the process that our suffering makes us stronger. We must have fortitude to withstand some of the challenges in life.

In 1 Peter 2, the unjust treatment of Christian slaves is described. Peter encouraged loyalty and endurance, even if the bad treatment was at the hand of their masters. In the same way, we should also abide the pain and hardship we face. We may suffer for many reasons. Some is a direct result of our sin; other adversity is the byproduct of living in a sinful world. Here, Peter writes about suffering as a result of doing good. Christ was sinless, yet He endured the death of the cross so that we could be set free.

We never know who is watching us. By following Christ's example of how to persist through distress, we can win others to Him. What suffering have you endured that has drawn another to the love of Christ? Remember—and rejoice in how God used you.

"Then what *are* you saying?"

"I really don't know," he said, straight-faced and impassive. "Maybe seventy percent."

I looked him straight in the eye. "My husband and I are both believers in God. I already have people all over the country praying for me. It's going to be one hundred percent."

Dr. Manning looked like a scientist; skeptical but respectful of my beliefs, though I had a feeling that he thought I was nuts. But I felt good about what I'd just said. It was the first time I had publically acknowledged what God told me about the testimony that was going to come out of this trial.

I just put it out there, I thought. *A declaration of life. Of faith in my God.*

When I woke up the next morning, I padded to the bathroom as usual to brush my teeth—and it all hit me. I started weeping—insistently, but not the "ugly cry" from earlier in the week. Barney heard me from the bedroom, and he was there in seconds.

"What's wrong?" he asked.

"I don't want to do this."

He came in front of me and firmly wrapped his arms around my shoulders.

"It's going to be okay."

We hugged a moment longer, and I absorbed his comfort. Then he went back to bed and I picked up my toothbrush. His words and his embrace were all I needed. That's fitting. It's always been that way.

Chapter Two

Hardly a day has passed without Barney Hilton Murray in my life. He's part of my earliest memories—understandable, since our parents were friends long before either one of us were born. Only one year and three days apart in age, Barney and I lived within a ten minute drive of each other in White Plains, New York, went to the same church, and attended the same public schools.

There was something different about Barney. His focus was not like other boys; while most were only interested in sports and girls, Barney set his eyes on hard work. He was quiet, studious and ambitious, with interests in photography, sports, music, and woodworking. To earn money, he worked in a small family-owned kitchen cabinet shop after school. I insisted on playing the flute in the fourth grade so I could be with him in the school band, where he was a drummer. We participated in children's activities together in church.

I saw Barney on weekdays after school. He often came over to my house to play with my brothers, and I'd hang nearby—either playing with my dolls in the yard or, as I grew older, joining them in a game of touch football. As kids, Barney and I were just friends, and not even close ones.

That started to change in high school. In the hallway between classes, I'd find my eyes drawn to him—and I'd feel a flutter whenever he returned my gaze. I kept this attraction to myself; after all, my brothers were still his friends, and I didn't need the teasing. Besides, it's not like we were boyfriend-girl-friend or anything. We dated once, if you want to call it that. It was on a school field trip to Manhattan to see the play Purly. All week leading up to the trip, my two best friends Rhonda and Lila joined me to plan our outfits and shoes and do our hair in anticipation. Barney and I sat next to each other on the bus and in the theater, but it seemed to me that I was the only one seeing this opportunity as a "date." Barney hardly said a word to me, and he didn't even sit next to me on the bus ride home to White Plains.

> "You know," I said, "I kinda liked you in high school."

I didn't think Barney was intentionally trying to ignore me. I supposed he just didn't see me as anything more than the girl he'd grown up with.

Then came another bus ride. It was a few years later when our church was visiting another congregation in Brooklyn. We once again found ourselves sitting together. We were college-aged by then and really hadn't seen much of each other since high school other than in church. I started with some chit-chat to get him talking, and gradually the conversation turned down memory lane.

"You know," I said, "I kinda liked you in high school."

He smiled. "You mean 'liked' liked?" He paused. "Well, I kinda liked you, too." We recalled the trip to Manhattan, and he revealed that he was so aloof then because he was nervous and didn't really know what to say to me. *Aha!* I thought. *So it was a date!*

After the church gathering, we sat together again on the return trip—and this time it was on purpose. We talked more and really started to click. As we neared our church, Barney asked me if I'd like to go out sometime to see a movie. We started dating, and then talking on the phone most every day. After literally a lifetime together, Barney and I were beginning to get to know each other as adults. There was Sunday dinner following watching afternoon football at his parent's home, Saturday dinner and movie dates, and Friday night TV time at my little studio apartment after church choir rehearsals. This went on for about a year. In all this time, though, he never gave me a kiss. Didn't even try—and, trust me, I gave him every opportunity.

One Friday night after rehearsal, we were watching Showtime at the Apollo. As usual, I had a fresh bowl of fruit and some snacks for us, and we sat on my couch arm-in-arm. It was about midnight when he got up to leave and, before we got to the door, Barney leaned in and gave me a kiss. After so many nights without one, it took me completely by surprise. *Ding-dong crash-bang-boom!* I heard bells and whistles and saw stars and fireworks! No kidding, it was the best kiss ever—tender but deep, all I'd ever dreamed it would be.

After he left, I pulled out the hide-a-bed and just lay there in la-la land. At that moment, I knew: Barney Hilton Murray was no longer just the boy I grew up with. I was in love. Two years later, we were married.

Barney received a job transfer with the IBM Corporation right before our wedding date, so the day after the reception we packed up and moved across country to the Bay Area of California, settling in San Jose. We found a new church home with Eastside Church of God in Christ and it was there, under the leadership of Sherman Harris, that I accepted a call from God to work in the ministry. I discovered God had created me with lead-

How to find and maintain genuine love in a marriage

That is why a man leaves his father and mother and is united to his wife, and they become one flesh. —Genesis 2:24

A good marriage starts with an understanding of the definition of marriage. Marriage was instituted by God and His plan consists of the man and woman becoming "one flesh," which includes physical and spiritual unity. Barney and I wanted our marriage to honor God and what He says about marriage. In His eyes, marriage is the earthly example of the relationship Jesus has with His bride, the church of Christian believers.

With God at the center of our marriage, we knew we had the answer to whatever problems we faced. We just had to ask Him. That wasn't always easy…we often let our own selfish desires get in the way. Ultimately, we got it together and turned to God. That practice helped prepare us to continue genuinely loving each other over thirty-five years later. Have we always had that twinkle in the eye for one another? Absolutely not. But we've always had God—and He has helped us to make it work.

Genuine love in a marriage equals God at the core of your relationship. If you didn't start off that way, it's not too late. The Lord is always willing and available to become the center of your marriage—and your entire life. Simply seek Him today.

ership and teaching gifts, and I already knew how much I loved to sing His praises.

By then, Barney and I had started a family. Aja was born in 1979; Aryn in 1982. We decided to raise our girls in church, mirroring the way we were brought up, and we desired for our children to learn about the plan of salvation through Jesus Christ as taught in the Bible. We also wanted them to develop a passion to lead others to a relationship with Jesus. As the children grew, they were active in school activities, Girl Scouts, sports, and the arts. At the same time, I developed my skills as administrator of the music department at Eastside, served in various leadership roles in the adult choir, and led the church praise and worship team. I also taught preschoolers in Sunday school and eventually became licensed as an Evangelist Missionary, or minister, of the Church of God in Christ, Inc.

In the meantime, Barney's work ethic from childhood served him well. He was a lab technician for IBM and a photographer on the side, hired for shoots at weddings and other special events. His garage was packed with woodworking tools and he made furniture, including a custom china cabinet for me and special pieces for each of the girls for their sixteenth birthdays. In church, he played keyboard, guitar, and drums, was the leader of the men's ministry, and taught Sunday school for senior high school boys, among other roles. Barney and I were a team in marriage, too, raising our daughters as a team and attending all but a handful of their creative arts or sports events over the years—all while managing the church-related work, which we did to a fault. I stopped working full-time when the girls were still in grade school. That made me available to spend more time with them and volunteer at school. I made a home-cooked dinner every night; we rarely ate out.

In 1997, we left Eastside to join Rod Simon, a longtime assistant pastor at the church and godfather of our daughters, as he started his own congregation, Life Community Church. The transition was smooth for us, but the start-up church was short lived. It shut its doors, and in 1999 we moved on to join Maranatha Christian Center under Pastor Tony Williams. I went right to work, becoming the facilitator for a women's small group Bible study and a mentor to young women. Barney and I also became the ministry leaders for married couples, meeting twice each month and imparting studies and activities to build healthy marriages on biblical principles. For the next six years, we had a great time. Eventually, Barney started his own woodworking business, and after working part-time for a friend who was a florist, I started my own in-home floral business. During this time, the girls became adults and moved away. Right before the big housing bust, we decided to try the market and sell our home. It sold in three days.

House sold, we had to figure what to do—and where to go—next. The choice to relocate to Tucson was obvious. Aryn had moved there to attend the University of Arizona. Aja joined her later, not to go to school, but to be closer to her sister. On a Thanksgiving visit to Tucson in 2005, Aja and her husband Glenn announced they were expecting our first grandchild. One month later, at Christmas, Aryn visited us in California and revealed that she, too, was pregnant.

That was all I needed. Nana mode kicked in and we made the move to the desert. Aja gave birth to a son, Aren Kai, in May 2006; Aryn had Arilàn DeLano, a girl, in July 2006. Aja and Glenn lived in Tucson while Aryn and Delawn dwelled in Phoenix, only a couple hours away to the northwest. I babysat Aren and visited Arilàn and family on weekends and holidays. I was in my early fifties, active and enjoying life. Other than having my tonsils removed and giving birth to my girls, I'd never spent a single day in the hospital.

Dr. Huerta told me I had cancer—and God told me that I would be healed of cancer—on October 29, 2007, and I knew I was about to become all-too-familiar with hospitals. Yet even before my first outpatient procedures in November to insert a stomach tube for nutrition and a port-a-catheter to receive my chemotherapy treatments, I made a decision. I was going to *live out* my faith during the arduous journey ahead. That meant I needed to walk like, act like, and look like I've already been healed. I expected to feel horrible, but I didn't have to be horrible, look horrible, or act horrible. I didn't want others to see the Jacki that was tired, weak, and losing weight. I wanted them to see God and say to themselves, "Either this lady is cuckoo, or there is something going on inside this woman. She has faith!"

> I made a decision. I was going to live out *my faith.*

I wanted to experience cancer with grace—God's grace shining through me—in my walk, my attire, my attitude. Everything.

My first chemotherapy treatment at the cancer center started on Friday, November 16. A pump was connected to me so I could self-administer doses of the medicine at home, and I returned the following Tuesday to have the pump disconnected. That was followed by sixteen days of rest and recovery from the first treatment before starting the next one on December 7. When I went in for my initial treatment, Barney and little Aren joined me along with an unexpected guest: my mother Margaret, all the way from Florida. She said she came to help—even though I'd told her not to come. I didn't know what kind of help, if any, that I was going to need. It's not that I have a bad relationship with my mother; I love her deeply and still call her Mommy. But I wanted to take care of myself and not have the extra responsibility of being a dutiful daughter when I was the one who was ill. Plus, I wanted the first treatment to be as non-dramatic as possible. I didn't know what to expect, I wasn't looking forward to it, and I was trying to approach it as just another doctor's visit.

When we checked in and took our seats in the waiting room, I couldn't help but sense I didn't belong. Most of the patients were elderly, and we were also the only African-Americans in the room. I was younger, I was darker, and it just felt weird. The awkwardness was exacerbated as we sat in silence while I filled out the paperwork. When my name was called, my mother, Barney, and even little Aren stood up to go back with me. "Nope," I said. "I want to do this by myself." Mommy's expression was a mix of surprise and disappointment. I knew she wanted to be the doting mother. More than anything, I simply desired to be alone. I was ushered into a small room so a nurse could take my vital signs, and then I was escorted into a large room with a nurse's station at the center and reclining chairs lined up all along the outside walls. I took a seat in one of the chairs. Another nurse came in, found her name on the white board, and checked it off; calm and routine, as I'm sure she had done every day for a long time.

She came over, smiled, and introduced herself. "I'm going to connect an IV to your catheter. We'll flush it first, then administer the medication, and flush it again. There will be two bags of fluid to empty. This will take three or four hours," she explained. "When it's done, I'll connect the catheter to the machine you'll take with you so you can continue the chemo at home through the weekend." It was pretty straightforward, so I had no questions.

She hooked me up and left me alone. I had my iPod and my journal to keep me occupied and, being me, I eventually struck up conversations with a couple of ladies who came in; one was a patient who'd had cancer twice before, the other a support group leader who told me about the support services available to me. That was funny, because I told her I was doing fine and that I was going to be healed. I ended up encouraging her when she was the one coming in to encourage me as a first-time cancer patient.

The treatment didn't hurt. Actually, there was no sensation at all as the clear, thin fluids flowed into my body.

Well, this is kinda cool! I thought. *This is like sitting in the beauty shop.* It certainly wasn't what I expected: I'd anticipated something more clinical and, well, painful.

As I left with my port-a-catheter, a small device about the size of an old rectangular cassette deck from Radio Shack, I looked at the shoulder bag they gave me to carry it in. It was labeled "Arizona Oncology," and I didn't like it because it further identified me as a cancer patient. Barney later purchased a nice Ralph Lauren bag for the machine, which I thought communicated a more positive message.

We got back home, and that evening Aja and Glenn came over to visit. I requested some Kentucky Fried Chicken mashed potatoes to satisfy a craving, and I felt great. We ate, hung out together as a family, and went to bed.

When I woke up the next morning, I felt like a car had smashed through my bedroom window and run me over. BAM! I was exhausted, as though I'd somehow just ran a marathon while doing the grocery shopping at the same time. *I have to get up and go to the bathroom*, I thought, *but I'm really too tired.* The doctors had told me, of course, that one of the side effects of chemotherapy would be fatigue. But this was beyond fatigue—and so soon. It was like there was a rhinoceros on top of me. I couldn't move. I certainly didn't want to.

Urged on by my bladder, I eventually made it to the bathroom, a tiny journey of a few feet from my bedside. It seemed to take an eternity. I brushed my teeth, washed my face, and headed into the family room. Mommy was still asleep, so I flopped onto the soft cushions of the sofa. I didn't move for the rest of the day.

The next morning was identical except for the added sensation of nausea. It wasn't the "I ate too much spicy food" type of nausea; this was the "I went on the Twist-A-Loop, then had a soda and cotton candy, then went on the Speed-a-Whirl, and then danced for hours in a circle" sort of nausea. It was unpleasant—and Mommy offered chicken broth to help with the nausea, but I had no appetite. I forced down about half a cup. So it remained that day, and the next, until I went in Tuesday to disconnect the pump. Nevertheless, that first Sunday evening, we did go to church for a special reason. Pastor Horace Sheppard, a longtime friend of Pastor Tony Williams in California, was in town from Philadelphia to hold a revival service. My mother and my sister Lori, who lives with my mom in Florida, joined Barney and me; I was excited to hear Pastor Sheppard and thrilled that I had sufficient strength to attend—and it was a good thing I did. During the portion of the service when the attendees are encouraged to meet and greet each other, the pastor of the church introduced himself to us. "I know one of you must be a singer," he said, "so be ready." Recognizing my cue, I felt an empty pit in my stomach that had nothing to do with the nausea from the chemo. *Sing? It's been so long since I sang because of the ear problem. I'm not prepared. I'm tired. Can I do it?* When the pastor called me up to the platform, God empowered my body and my courage. I shared about my cancer, and included the revelation that this

Why you can sing to the Lord, even in your suffering

Shout for joy, you heavens; rejoice, you earth;
burst into song, you mountains!
For the Lord comforts his people and will
have compassion on his afflicted ones. —Isaiah 49:13

Music has always played an important role in my life. Growing up, my siblings and I all learned to play instruments and I also sang. We played in the school band and I was in our high school chorus. I was even a part of a rhythm and blues group during my teenage years.

When I made a serious decision with walk with the Lord, my singing became a form of worship. I realized that being able to sing is more than a talent, performance, or entertainment. It's a gift from God. You may not have the perfect voice or tone, but when you use your voice to worship God, it is a sweet sound to His ear. Singing that is performance-driven is focused on the singer. Singing that is worship-driven is focused on God. Therefore, even during suffering, the song is not about you. It's about Him.

When you're afflicted, you can sing "How Great is Our God" because regardless of what you are going through, *He* is still great! And surprisingly, focusing on God when you sing makes the suffering a little easier to endure. So sing to the Lord a new song—for He is good, and He will comfort you.

would be the first time I'd sung for anyone in months. Barney sat down at the keyboard and started playing, and I sang "His Eye is on the Sparrow." To my amazement, I could hear myself; not fully, but far better than I had since the summer. I received a nice ovation, too, so I must've been reasonably in tune.

If that wasn't joy enough, Pastor Sheppard called Barney and I forward to receive prayer after he finished his message. As he prayed, he said, "The cancer you have is rare because it will be something for you to minister from. It's for ministry," he repeated. "It's for ministry." It was an unexpected but encouraging confirmation of what the Lord had already spoken to me. As it turned out, that was one of the last church services I'd be able to attend for a while, but it was significant.

From then on, each day was a grind of getting up, sitting on the couch, watching TV when I wasn't playing with Aren—or, better stated, *watching* Aren play since I had no energy—and trying but failing to eat. The feeding tube into my stomach was in place, but I didn't want to use it. When I finally did choose to use it, it fed me formula, similar to the kind given to babies, two ounces at a time. Needless to say, I lost weight speedily after treatments began. That first week after my first chemo treatment, my dental work also began that needed to be completed before I could start radiation treatments on my face, and we had no dental insurance and no extra money to cover the expenses. The Bible shares a simple yet powerful principle: ask, and it shall be given. I sat down at my computer and went to my email:

> *If you are receiving this email it's because I'm asking for your help. We are struggling financially and I have a major expense facing me. I have to have dental work done before I can begin my radiation treatments—which*

they want me to start as soon as possible. The dentist says that I need five crowns done, each costing $733. We do not have dental insurance and the work must be done now...not spread over a couple of months. So, I'm asking if you can send anything to help. It would be so appreciated. I know times are hard for everyone, so if you're not able, I definitely understand. Thank you so much!!!

I also knew I needed people to fulfill another biblical truth: knock, and it shall be opened. I prayed and God gave me the names of ten incredible women—my "sistah girls" who were powerful prayer warriors and filled with godly sass. I knew they would literally bombard Heaven on my behalf until they got an answer. These women lived in different parts of the country; they weren't personal friends, but they knew of each other. I also knew that they knew God, and that I could share the nastiest details of my sickness with them and they wouldn't be shaken. When I didn't have the energy to pray for myself, I knew they would be praying for me.

> *My personal intercessory team—my "PIT Crew" of prayer.*

Sandra, Davita, Della, Andrea, Elaine, Nellie, Clara, Carolynn, Lorinda, and Yvette. My personal intercessory team—my "PIT Crew" of prayer.

I started sending them regular emails on my condition, and they prayed for my complete healing, for the treatments to not be as harsh, for Barney and our marriage, for our daughters and their families, for our finances—you name it, they prayed it. Yvette even initiated a weekly prayer conference call with the group held every Monday evening at 6:00 p.m. It was an honor and incredibly strengthening to know these women were praying, fasting, and shouting my name and my needs to our great God.

I also received a phone call from another longtime friend, Debra, after the first email send. Years earlier, Debra had been very ill, and during that time God led me to call her daughter Tanisha twice a day for six weeks to talk with her and encourage her through Debra's illness. During that time Tanisha and I became close friends even though we were quite different in personality, such an odd couple that she nicknamed me Lady Felix while I dubbed her Oscarrah.

Now Debra wanted to return the favor. "You were there for my daughter," she told me, "and now I want to be there for you. I'm going to call you every Saturday morning." She did each weekend at eight o'clock sharp. She ended each call with, "I love you. Is there anything you need?" I always responded with, "I love you, too. No, I'm good." On her third call, Debra said, "You always say you don't need anything, but I think you do. So I'm going to do what the Lord is telling me. I'm going to send you one hundred dollars every two weeks out of my paycheck." She did—and her help met one need after another that otherwise would've been impossible to pay for. Every gift of financial help received in the weeks to come confirmed that God really does meet my needs; it's not just something I read in my Bible. I guess I didn't fully understand this because up until now I'd never been in true financial trial. It was awesome to watch God provide time and again through my friends, His people.

As we counted down toward Thanksgiving, Mommy thought it would be a good idea for me to call and ask Martha Houston to come stay with us. That's ironic, because Martha was like a second mom to me. She'd been in my life ever since Barney and

I moved to California from New York many years earlier. Martha was newly widowed when we met her, and she was raising four children on her own—but that didn't stop her from fully adopting our family into her fold. Martha was the woman who taught me how to raise my girls, how to be a wife, and even how to cook. We either saw, or spoke to each other over the phone, every day. We were active together at Eastside Church of God in Christ, and our families ate together almost every Sunday. Aja and Aryn were school-aged girls before they learned that their "Auntie Martha" and "Sister Houston" were the same person. There are no words to describe what Martha means to me, and I missed her desperately after we moved from California to Arizona. So, even though I knew it was a last-minute request, I gave in to Mommy's relentless pestering and called Martha. She left her family and came to spend her Thanksgiving with us; good thing, since she, Aja, and my cousin Germaine ended up doing all the cooking.

The evening after Martha arrived, I thought I felt strong enough after the outpatient procedures to have the feeding tube and port-o-cath inserted to take a shower. In my weakness, the flow of the water over my body was revitalizing. Then I turned the faucet off and reached to get a towel to dry off—and everything went black. Next thing I know, Barney was kneeling at my side. I was on the floor of the tub. I'd passed out.

"Are you okay, Jacki? Jacki?"

"I think so," I replied. "Help me up." He did, and I stepped out of the tub, he helped me dry off, and then I steadied myself in front of the sink. I looked in the mirror. Nothing seemed damaged. I nodded to my husband. "I'll be alright. Just let me finish getting ready." No sooner had he turned to leave that I went down again. I must've been out for mere seconds, but this time Barney was already helping me up when I came to.

"Let's get you to the bed," he said, and he helped me onto the mattress. I sat up, marveling at how I could feel okay one instant and be unconscious the next. With my mother around, the last thing I wanted to do was make a fuss, so I asked Barney, "Could you go ask Martha what I should do?" I thought maybe my blood sugar was too low.

He turned to leave, and I suddenly realized something rather obvious. "Wait! Can you get me some clothes first?" I was sitting there buck naked, a minor fact Barney didn't even seem to notice. I remained there in the buff for several more minutes as Barney struggled to find a pair of jammies that fit comfortably with my protruding stomach tube. By the time he came back with Martha I was feeling stronger and so we decided against a late night urgent care visit.

Thanksgiving Day arrived and everyone was there—Barney, Aja and Aryn and their families, my mother and sister, and even my cousin Germaine from New Jersey came after talking to me on the phone and saying she didn't like how I sounded.

My first thought was, *This is great! We're gonna have a big party!*

And it was, with two notable exceptions. Because her house was bigger than mine, dinner was going to be at Aja's home, though much of the food was prepared in advance at my house. As we got ready to head over to Aja's, Mommy took a seat on my sofa. "I'm not going," she said.

"What do you mean 'You're not going?' What's wrong?"

She didn't say and I couldn't figure it out, so I let her be and we left. The wonderful aromas of turkey, honey-baked ham, cornbread dressing, collard greens, black-eyed peas with ham hock,

Why it is important to be thankful in the midst of your trials

Let the peace of Christ rule in your hearts,
since as members of one body you were called to peace.
And be thankful. —Colossians 3:15

Peace and thankfulness? In the middle of the most horrific time of my life? Surely, you must be joking. Peace is defined as "freedom of the mind from annoyance, distraction, anxiety, an obsession; a state of tranquility or serenity." Yet trying to obtain peace based on society's definition can seem impossible. Peace doesn't mean that suddenly problems are eliminated. Cancer was still a reality. But I knew I had to embrace the peace of God as I took this journey.

Paul tells us to let Christ's peace be the ruler (or director) in our hearts, in the very center of our emotions where our feelings and desires clash between extremes—fear and hope, suspicion and trust, jealousy and love. It's impossible to constantly deal with these conflicts and live as God desires for us. We must allow the rule of His peace to settle the discord.

Let the peace of God be the director of your heart. It is then that you will be thankful, at peace—and maybe even able to have a party—during times of chaos and confusion.

macaroni and cheese, and sweet potato pie and fresh pound cake pleasantly but brutally assaulted my senses when we arrived, but I determined that no matter how awful I was feeling, I was going to try to eat. I could only get a few bites down, though; it hurt so bad I could barely swallow, much less keep anything down. Sadly, the babies ate more than me; they were perched in their high chairs around the long dining room table, the only ones denied access to the special china set out for the occasion. I was both mad and sad about my inability to eat, yet that was offset by the joy of being with all these loving people—my family! I didn't think once about Mommy or how she was doing.

When we got home late that night, we found her—still sitting on the sofa in the pitch dark. She hadn't moved a muscle, and that included doing nothing about the disarray left over from the day's earlier activities in the kitchen.

"Mommy?" I asked, feeling my frustration at not being able to eat transferring to a more immediate irritation. "Why are you still sitting here in the dark? And what's on the television, anyway?" It was CNN and she hates news, so it made no sense she would be watching that channel. "Why didn't you clean the kitchen?"

"Well, I didn't make the mess. It wasn't mine to take care of."

My internal pot went from simmer to full boil. "I thought you were here to help me!"

Looking back, I don't recall the rest of the argument, except that it was heated and reminiscent of every other argument her and I had ever had in our years together. Yet in my anger and tiredness, I discerned that something else—something significant and unknown to me—was terribly wrong. Much later, and to my regret, I realized Mommy was mourning both the loss of my brother Tracy, who'd died three years earlier just days before Thanksgiving, and the potential loss of me to the cancer.

Mommy's generation was private and simply didn't speak of such things. To this day, she has not said a word about it. That's just who she is.

That weekend, most everyone stayed to keep me company. No one fussed over me more than they should've done, even when one of my temporary crowns fell out. Since it was a holiday weekend, I went in to an alternate office recommended by my regular dentist. After explaining my situation, they replaced the crown for no additional charge. It was the start of a financial miracle from God. In the days following my email request about the five crowns, people responded with one hundred dollars here, another couple of hundred there, until we had received about one-third of the total needed. It was wonderful! Then Barney received a call from one of the recipients; she was checking in on how I was feeling. Near the close of the conversation, she said, "Oh, by the way, tell Jacki I got her email, and I'm sending something to help."

Two days later, we received a card from her. Barney opened it first, read it, and just stared at it, his expression utterly blank. He then handed the card to me and I opened it. Out fell a check for the entire amount: $3,665. In its weakness, my body wouldn't allow it—so I just imagined myself doing a little happy dance right there in our living room. *Okay, God,* I thought. *You've got this!*

On November 30, Aja came over for her usual Friday night visit. I was sitting on the couch across from her when my scalp suddenly felt as though someone had taken a hot curling iron and rolled it across my skin, singeing everything in its path. I reached up in response to this sudden burning sensation and ran my fingers

> Okay, God,
> I thought.
> You've got this!

through my hair. When my hand came down I looked at it, like it was something alien. It was full of black strands. I repeated the process, hand up and back down, and it came out in clumps that I carefully stacked on the end table. Aja curled her lip and leaned back in her chair. Her face had a pained expression. "Mom? Do you have to make a pile of hair?" I guess it bothered her to see it, but what else could I do? She used to be a cosmetologist, so when there was nothing left on my head but tufts, I asked her to use Barney's barber shears and she finished the job faster than I expected. I was completely bald. It'd only taken a few minutes.

Not long after losing my hair, I received an email with a picture attached to it. It was from my "niece" Alyse Calhoun. She's the daughter of my best friend Lisa. Alyse and I developed a special relationship during the time I babysat her at age four. The picture was of her; she had shaved off all of her hair in honor of me.

My shiny dome was on full display when I went in the following week for my second of three scheduled chemotherapy treatments on Friday, December 7. Like before, I had the pump connected for at-home treatments and needed to return the following Tuesday to have the pump removed before another sixteen-day recovery period. The visit itself was routine, but that weekend was brutal. I was far more ill than with my first treatment. When I had to go from my bed to the bathroom, I literally had to crawl the short distance.

By the start of the following week it was mid-December, the time I usually started my Christmas decorating. Christmas had always been a big deal; when I was a little girl in New York, we usually went to Rockefeller Center to see the giant tree, skate on the ice rink, and take in the festive sights. As an adult, I was that person who made sure the wrapping paper matched the ornaments on the tree and created a home that was bright and regal. I even have a lead crystal Nativity set. On top of that, Christmas was always a busy but thrilling time at church; there were always services to attend and presentations to rehearse. But this year, I was drained physically and felt almost as empty spiritually. God had me in a dry, desert land. Everything about me had changed. I had no control over any of it. So I didn't do squat for Christmas. I didn't miss the decorating or the shopping; I didn't care about the glitter and glitz. Aryn agreed to host the family for Christmas at her home in Phoenix, and that was fine by me. I just wanted to get through to the radiation treatments scheduled to begin the first week of January.

I went in to see Dr. Ketchel and received some unexpected good news: the tumor had shrunk enough from the first two chemo treatments that I wouldn't need a third. However, it was now time to get the CT scan needed as the final step before radiation. I arrived at the cancer center December 18 and was prepped to be placed into the tube. As I lay on my back, I was told the procedure would only take five minutes, and I took a deep breath of relief. Then a mesh mask was placed over my face. A chemical was added to help the mesh melt over my eyes, nose, and mouth. It was warm, and while I could still see and breathe through the mesh, I could feel it tightening to my skin. I was slid head first into the tube and heard the *whacka-whacka-whacka* of the machine. In mere moments, my anxiety peaked. My breathing was raspy, my muscles tensed, and my arms at my side pressed downward onto the platform. I was certain the walls of the cylinder were squeezing inward, poised to smother me. I let out a scream, raw and primal.

"Get me out!"

The technician responded, his voice ridiculously calm. "Mrs.

Murray. You only need another minute-and-a-half and you'll be finished."

"I don't care! Get me out—now!"

The narrow slab all-too-slowly slid out of the tube. The mask was pulled aside and, after calling Dr. Manning for permission, I was given a Xanax in an attempt to sedate my frazzled nerves. It didn't work. The technician received word that an emergency patient had just arrived, and that the machine was needed. "We have to put you back in, Mrs. Murray."

My resolve was firm. "No."

"If you don't finish now, you're going to have to leave and come back."

"Then I'm leaving."

I did return that afternoon, again enduring the mask and finishing the final ninety seconds. To this day, that remains one of the most frightening events of my entire life.

On December 22, I received a surprise guest for Christmas—my friend Clara or, as I call her, Clara Belle. Originally from North Carolina, she still speaks with that lovely southern drawl, even after years living in California. She was part of one of my Bible study groups from my West Coast days, and I became a friend whom she could trust and with whom she could share her most personal needs. Even though we did nothing more than hang out at the house in the days leading up to Christmas, it was a joy to be with her again. The only time we did venture out was on Christmas Eve. She insisted on doing some gift shopping for the babies even though I told her she didn't need to do so, and then we went to Chick-Fil-A for my favorite milkshake. As we sat and chat, I was distracted by a woman who kept looking at me from across the dining room. It wasn't until we left and I noticed my reflection in the glass door that I figured out why she was

What do you do when fear comes upon you?

So don't be afraid; you are worth more than many sparrows. —Matthew 10:31

Fear can be crippling, even paralyzing. It can stop everything you try to accomplish. Imagine being told you have a fatal disease, or that a significant person in your life has suddenly died, or finding a pink slip on your desk when you arrive at work? There are so many events that happen in our lives that are totally out of our control—and some of them are scary! It's human nature to feel a certain level of fear in these moments.

Here in Matthew, Jesus teaches that God's children are valuable to their Father. He knows everything that happens to even the little sparrows, so He absolutely knows all about our troubles! He knows every fear we face, every doubt we entertain. He values us enough to send Jesus to die on the cross. We are never away from His thoughts, care, or presence.

Through your relationship with the Lord, you will experience His undying care and love. I can't promise you that fear, worry, and doubt won't creep in. But I can promise that you don't have to remain under their influence as you remember how valuable you are to Him.

looking at me so often. *Oh yeah…I'm bald.* I was so used to it by then I never gave it a thought. After leaving, we we stopped at the grocery store on the way home. As we walked down the frozen food aisle, I felt a tap on my shoulder.

It was a different lady. She was cheery as could be, and she acted like she'd known me her entire life. "Can I give you a hug?" she asked.

It's not often you get asked that question, especially at the store. I didn't know what to say. *This woman's awfully happy, but I don't know her.* "Uh—sure."

She took me into her arms, and then pulled away. "I just want to let you know it's gonna be okay," she said. She must've seen my scrunched up forehead, so she clarified. "All of my hair grew back."

Oh, I thought, reminded again of my baldness. *She must've had cancer in the past.* "Oh, it's just a process I'm going through," I offered. "I already know I'm healed."

Her face beamed. "Amen, sister!" Then she walked away. I never saw her again. If she would've walked up to me again five minutes later, I don't believe I would've recognized her. She wasn't an angel in the literal sense. But I know God sent her to me.

The next morning, we drove up to Aryn's and watched the babies open all their presents. I laughed at how they were far more interested in ripping and eating the wrapping paper than in the toys they received. My energy was decent and the day was nice and low-key. We drove home that night, and Clara went back home to California two days later. That left me in a bit of a funk. My circle of friends, with me more or less every day since before Thanksgiving, was gone. Chemotherapy was finished, but radiation was looming ahead. It was a dreary in-between place.

Aja and Aryn noticed and decided to start planning a party for my birthday on January 20. They didn't share any details, except to say they were going to invite more of my dear out-of-state friends to attend.

That lifted my spirits and gave me just enough momentum at the advent of a new year to head into the next benchmark in my journey—and one of the most difficult.

Chapter Thr

Eight years earlier, everybody was freaking out on New Year's Eve. I actually knew of people who had raided the grocery store shelves and stocked up on batteries, bottled water, and canned goods, convinced that the planet that was going to shut down at the stroke of midnight. For many, Y2K was a legitimate, all-consuming fear of the future.

Perhaps I should've felt that same fear as I rose out of bed on December 31, 2007 and got ready to go in for the first of thirty-one days of radiation treatments. Like Y2K, I'd been told what to expect, but I had no idea what the actual reality was going to be like. There would be two treatments a day, one in the morning and another in the afternoon, every weekday for six weeks, with a final day added at the end. Each time, I'd have to wear my mesh mask. The treatments wouldn't hurt, but the aftermath could be more difficult than anything I'd experienced up to that point with the chemotherapy.

As I got dressed, I thought back to my commitment to live out my faith—to walk like, act like, and look like I've already been healed, and to experience cancer with grace. I went to my wardrobe and found a nice outfit and matching set of shoes. I couldn't wear makeup or jewelry on my head because that was where the radiation was going to be administered, but I could doll myself up from the neck down. I wanted to feel and look like princess. Most of all, I longed to shake off the shackles of y post-holiday blues. I was determined to be fierce and fearless. The Queen Diva.

Barney drove me to the cancer center. Check in was the same as before with the chemotherapy treatments, but instead of receiving an IV, I was given a chemo shot. I was told the medicine was going to be sufficient for both daily treatments, and I had no doubt that it was true, the syringe was so huge. Next, I went downstairs to the radiation department and to a small changing room where I could leave my purse. Because my head was being treated, I didn't have to undress or put on a hospital gown. A few minutes later, I was led into a huge, dimly-lit room with an exam table and massive robotic apparatus in the center. A windowed-off room, like those seen attached to interrogation rooms in crime dramas, was in the back. It was bright and contained computer consoles and other equipment. Two technicians came out from there to greet me, and they directed me toward the table. I saw my mask and a little lump of a pillow positioned to support my neck.

> I was determined to be fierce and fearless. The Queen Diva.

"Just lie down on your back, Mrs. Murray."

I did as I was told. The surface was rigid with the thinnest of a cushion, and as I tried to shimmy my torso into a comfortable position, the mask was placed over my face—and snapped to the table. I took an involuntary gasp. Then one of the techs took my arms, laid them flat to each side of me, and strapped down my wrists. That took me by surprise. *What are you doing?*

As if in response to my unspoken query, the tech said, "It's very important, Mrs. Murray, that you be in the exact same position every time so that the radiation will be administered correctly. Most people tend to cross their arms or their ankles. We do this so that won't happen, and the treatment can be finished as quickly as possible." Then she fastened my ankles to the table in confirmation of her words.

Despite feeling like Frankenstein on the slab, I kept my cool, resigned to my fate. But when the two techs left to go into the little windowed room, I felt my pulse quicken. My mind told me they were right there next door, but with my head pinned down I couldn't see them. *I'm alone.* I'd always hated that sense of being alone and trapped. One of my earliest childhood memories took place when I was three years of age. My parents were buying a new house in New York. During the move, they sent my little brother and me to stay with my aunt in Philadelphia. She lived in the projects, so whenever she went away to run a quick errand, she locked us away in a bedroom. I know she did it to keep us safe, and I remember I wasn't terrified per se, but I was frightened. The trigger of that memory swam back to life as I lay there. *I'm all by myself, and I can't move.*

Suddenly I saw red laser beams shoot from somewhere off the walls, and the big machine started gliding above my head in response, apparently to get in just the right alignment. I'm sure my eyes bulged beneath my mesh veil. The machine maneuvered itself so that its lens settled close to the right side of my head. Then I saw a harsh, flat light and heard an electronic *bzzzzz.* It stopped and the machine moved directly over my head. *Bzzzzz.* Then to the left. *Bzzzzz.* I thought the light blasted a tad longer on my right side, which made sense since that's where the largest of the three tumors was located. Moments later, the techs came in, deftly unstrapped my legs and arms and removed the mask—and I was done. I didn't feel anything: no heat, no pain. The treatment itself took less time than it did to strap me to the table.

I went home, and then returned at 4:00 p.m. for the exact same process. That night, Barney and I decided to go to a New Year's Eve Watch Night Service. It was my first time in church since the service with Pastor Sheppard right after my chemo started. I was looking forward to it; in California, Watch Night services were more like Holy Ghost parties filled with high praise. This service, however, was dull in comparison and I was a tad disappointed. Still, it was a good way to ring in the New Year, and I counted my blessings.

The next week of treatments went fine, and I wasn't feeling nearly as ill as I thought I would. In an attempt to make up for what I felt I was missing by not attending church, I listened to hours of Christian music and sang along to orchestrate my own personal worship time. I found myself remembering the truth of Scripture that was hidden in my heart. I sensed I had to rely on the Word that I knew—and on the powerful, healing God it declared. As I slowly nourished myself out of my spiritual desert, I stayed as active as possible. Each day I got out of bed, took a shower, made the bed, and then rested a moment before getting dressed. Then I went to the living room, sat on the couch, and watched television, babysat little Aren or, as the radiation treatments progressed, took naps. I talked on the phone and checked my emails when I had the energy.

I also benefitted from the love and care of two special neighbors who couldn't have been more different from each other or from me. Bo lives two doors down from me; Diana lives right across the street from her. Bo is eccentric, quirky, and kinda weird; she wears mismatching socks just because she wants to. That's what makes her so cool—that, and she's an old fashioned neighbor, the kind of person that I could sit down with in my bathrobe and have a cup of tea (or, in Bo's case, coffee with hazelnut

How to rest in the truth of God's Word

Trouble and distress have come upon me, but your commands give me delight. —Psalm 119:143

Pleasure can be found in the Word of God. Following the simple truths of the Word can provide comfort in difficult times. The Word of God doesn't promise that we will never endure pain and heartache. We live in a sinful world; therefore, we will suffer, sometimes without explanation.

Cancer is not the worst thing I've experienced in my life. There have been many other instances where I have felt distress, pain, and heartache. But I've learned to trust in the Word of God and "ride the tide." His Word tells me that He will never leave me nor forsake me. So through the pain, I know He's there. When I feel like I've cried the very last tear, I know He's there. When I feel like I've reached the very end of my rope, I know He's there!

God's Word is limitless. It is for all people throughout all time. It's not a book of history stories that are not applicable today. When Heaven and Earth pass away, God's Word will remain; the commands of the Lord recorded in His Word still hold true—right now, in the midst of your suffering.

So find delight in His commands and promises. They will be your rest in the roughest of times.

cream). Diana is a single mom who keeps more to herself; not shy, but reserved. She's not so much a "come on over and hang out" kind of person, but she's the one who will pick up the newspaper or get the mail when I'm away. Diana also does my nails at her at-home salon. Both ladies have keys to the house. As far as faith is concerned, the subject has never come up with Diana and me, but years later Diana told me that she was terrified during the time I was sick because she thought I was going to die. She often wept and prayed, she said, and revealed that she didn't visit as much as she wanted because it was devastating to her to see me so ill and she didn't want to upset me by crying.

Bo expressed to me that she doesn't believe in God, but from the very beginning, I told Bo that I believed God was going to heal me. I wasn't preachy about it; that isn't the kind of relationship we have. Instead I told her, "I have cancer, but I'm not keeping it." Every few days, she stopped by just to chitchat. Sometimes I fell asleep in the middle of the conversation, but she never minded. I was just as liable to find her still sitting there when I woke up, comforting me with her presence. Yet even when she went home, I knew she'd be back later or on another day, always ready to give me the gift of herself. Later, Bo told me she kept a little piece of paper with my name on it in her pocket. She often touched it, saying it was her way of keeping me close to her heart.

A few days into the second week of radiation, I started having trouble with getting strapped down for the treatments. I even panicked a couple of times and needed to get up from the table and return to the waiting room. Sometimes Barney prayed with me; other times I just sat for a moment to settle my nerves. The techs were accommodating, but they were also clear that I couldn't stay away long, and I certainly couldn't leave. The daily schedule was tight, and other patients had to be seen. I relied on my Xanax prescription of one or two pills prior to leaving the house to take the edge off my anxiety. I also drew relief later that week from my scheduled manicure appointment at Diana's house. Diana is covered in tattoos, but the body art is just the deceptively tough exterior for the sweetest lady I know. In the past, I walked to her home for my manicures, but this time I drove there. I was simply too tired to make the short trek on foot. Sadly, I was even too pooped to talk while Diana polished and buffed. I knew that would be okay, though. Diana's caring for me surpassed conversation. She was also aware of my declaration of faith. Right after diagnosis, I told her God was going to heal me. "Okay," she said, not derogatorily but supportively. "That sounds good to me."

My strength started draining even more by the third week, and when it did, it plummeted. I had zero energy, even after getting a full night's sleep. Most of the time, I still chose to drive myself to my afternoon treatments. I remember one trip when I made it no further than a few blocks away from the house. I pulled over at a corner gas station, parked, open the car door, and threw up in the parking lot. I was barely back into the driver's seat when my phone rang. It was Barney.

"Whatcha doing?" He was downright chipper.

I added as much steel to my voice as I could muster. "I'm on my way to the cancer center."

"That's good," he responded, fooled by my upbeat tone. "How are you feeling?"

"I'm okay."

It was a bold-faced lie, I know—but I wanted to protect the little freedom I felt I had to make those drives to and from the treatments. If I could help it, I didn't want anyone else taking care of me. Perhaps I should've been more honest and less stubborn with Barney. As the days of radiation wore on, we started a wonderful nighttime ritual. As we went to bed, I got under the covers and, almost always, took a deep breath, thankful to have made it through another day.

"So how was your day?" he'd ask. We wouldn't talk about the radiation or anything having to do with treatments, but I'd tell him about everything else, and he was a great listener. Then I'd take my turn. "And how was your day?" He'd tell me about work and anything else that he'd done that day. It was simple, mundane, caring conversation; we were twenty-eight years into our marriage—and we'd never done that before! *That little knucklehead boy I grew up with is still right here by my side*, I thought, *going through this with me. Wow, God!* We were experiencing intimacy at a level we never had before in our busy, responsibility-laden, church-filled lives. It was wonderful!

> We started a wonderful nighttime ritual.

Another delightful surprise was my birthday party—and the girls outdid themselves. They chose a Disco theme, complete with full-on psychedelic costumes and music from the decade. Aja and Aryn went out and bought me a completely rad blouse, splashed with color, and hoop earrings to match. Barney, of course, decked himself out in a button-up silk shirt with a giant collar. Plunged into the corner of the icing on the cake was a little plastic disco dancer. It was a riot, and it was made all the more fun by the friends who had showed up from out of town: Davita from Boston, Janice and Della from California, and Lisa from Atlanta. Bo and her boyfriend Doug were also there. Everyone was wearing a big Afro wig, and all of my favorite foods were on hand, and while I couldn't eat any of them, I didn't mind. The party was at Aja's house and I wore myself out, but when it was time to go back home, I didn't want it to end. We kept it going as late as possible before I conked out for the night. Della, who had to drive all the way from southern California with her three boys for the party, told me a story about her sons Brian and Landin, our godchildren along with her other son Andrew. Six-year-old Brian was praying at bedtime with four-year-old Landin, and declared he was going to pray for his Auntie Jacki.

"Well," Landin responded, "I'm going to pray for Uncle Barney."

"Why do you want to do that?" Brian countered. "Auntie Jacki has the cancer."

"Yeah," he said, "but Uncle Barney sleeps with her, and I want to pray that he doesn't catch cancer from her."

My party was followed by another pair of blessings. The first was a suitcase full of beautiful clothes—slacks, dresses, suits, blouses, jackets, scarves—that arrived courtesy of Andrea and Charles. These friends lived in California but were visiting an investment property in Chandler, Arizona south of Phoenix. When Janice, who had been to my party and seen my dramatic weight loss, heard that Andrea and Charles were coming to Arizona, she gave them that suitcase full of clothes that fit my now decidedly smaller frame, and they drove down to Tucson to make the delivery. It was yet another example of God taking care of my needs through my friends. As my radiation treatments continued, the second blessing came through my chitchat relationship with Margaret, a fellow patient who was receiving treatments because of breast cancer. She completed her treatments earlier than I did, so after her last treatment, Margaret departed the clinic before I was done but left behind a card. Next to a drawing of a paisley yellow flower, the front of the sky blue card read, "Your strength may surprise you." Inside, written in lovely cursive, were these words: *While I don't know you well, you have dignity and grace ... you have the capacity to see beyond yourself ... you are a strong but serene woman ... you would be a wonderful friend.* I only saw Margaret once a week, maybe for no more than five minutes at a time. It reminded me that I never know who is watching me or who I'm going to touch.

Despite those encouragements, I was feeling worse than ever. After a particularly severe anxiety attack during treatment, I went in to see Dr. Manning. He suggested I make a special trip to the cancer center to get hydrated. Lisa was still in town for a few extra days, so she joined me. We're very best friends despite being total opposites; Lisa is pencil-thin, quirky, and a deep thinker who loves to ask, "Have you ever thought about...?" She accompanied me back into the treatment room and wanted to know all the details about what it was like to get chemotherapy, radiation, the whole works. It was like she was interviewing me for an in-depth magazine article. However, I wanted to talk about anything *but* cancer, and I was exhausted—so I suppose it shouldn't have surprised Lisa that I fell asleep on her in mid-conversation. When I woke up, I was too woozy to walk on my own, so Lisa helped me out into the waiting room. It must've looked funny; her Olive Oyl frame trying to hold up my more Bluto-like physique, and neither one of us having a Popeye to help. We managed, though, to get me home.

Sadly, that was not going to be my last extra visit to the center. I didn't improve, and after a second appointment with Dr. Manning, he diagnosed me with severe dehydration. He decided to postpone my fifth week of radiation treatments so I could add four more days of sessions to get fully rehydrated. On February 8, I met with Dr. Manning again, and he cleared me to resume receiving radiation. I had only six days left to complete, but I

How to equip yourself to be His light to the world

In the same way, let your light shine before others,
that they may see your good deeds and glorify
your Father in heaven. —Matthew 5:16

I will always remember the first sentence of the book *The Purpose Driven Life* by Rick Warren: It's not about you. What? We always want it to be about us. If it's something good, we want to draw attention to ourselves and receive accolades and applause. If it's something bad, we want pity, tolerance, and forgiveness. Yet it should never be about us. When we allow His light to shine through us, everything we experience in life will point others towards Him.

Matthew compares followers of Christ to a lamp. We should be like a light which, if it is going to fulfill its function, must be on a stand and not hidden. If we live for God, our light—Christ—will glow bright for all to see. Then we won't attract men to ourselves but instead compel them to glorify the Father in Heaven.

Don't shut your light off from the rest of the world. Immerse yourself in prayer, the Bible, and worship, and you'll be a beacon of His truth!

shared my worry about going back in and being strapped to the table. Knowing it was temporary, he recommended I up my daily Xanax intake, and I gladly obliged. It made the difference, and the final twelve sessions came and went. On February 15, I had my final treatment—and it was the best TGIF of my life! That night, Aja and Glenn stopped by the house for their usual Friday night visit. As we had dinner, I was both excited and nervous. I was anxious because I was now starting an eight-week-long wait before I'd know if the cancer was completely gone, but thrilled that I was finally going to start feeling better with the end of the radiation.

The reality was that my body still needed time to recover, but my brain told me the radiation was over—so it was time to get on with living! That's why on Saturday I decided to go grocery shopping by myself. I drove to the store near my home and followed my usual methodical course through the store. I reveled in once again pushing the cart down one aisle and then up the next, making my selections and enjoying the simple pleasure of independence. Nevertheless, as I neared the end of my journey, I was standing at the deli counter poised to head to the checkout line when, all of a sudden, I felt woozy.

No, it was more than woozy. I was ready to pass out.

I looked around the nearby produce section. I considered the bins holding the fresh fruit and vegetables. *If I just walked over and collapsed into the granny smiths for a moment, I wonder if anyone would notice?* I decided there was no appropriate place for a swoon and gathered my strength. By the time I leaned into my cart enough to wheel it to the nearest register, one of the workers ushered me over to another newly opened line.

"I'm not doing so well," I told him, trying not to panic him or myself. "Can you move my cart out of line so I can sit a moment?"

I motioned toward the bench at the front of the store by the entrance. The mere nod of my head sent my senses swimming.

"Let me check all of your groceries for you while you wait," he offered, and I meandered over to the bench. When he was done, I made my way back over to him to make payment. He then asked if I

> It was time
> to get on
> with living!

wanted help getting everything to my car. "Oh, I'm doing fine." It was the exact same fib I'd told Barney weeks earlier. "Thank you," and with that I walked outside. I stopped again at another bench for a breather before managing to get to the car, load my bags, and drive home.

Ha! I did it! Then my brain added, *But that was pretty dumb, Jacki.*

I didn't tell Barney I made the trip alone, simply wanting to avoid his rebuke. Besides, I'd do better next time. After all, my radiation was over, and that tiny blister I noticed on the lower part of the right side of my neck was not going to dissuade me. Even after the blister had blossomed to cover my entire neck by bedtime, it didn't change my mindset. The pain from the blisters was excruciating when I woke up the next morning. Barney was getting ready for church.

I groaned quietly as I turned my head on the pillow. "About how long before you're ready to go?" I asked.

"Thirty minutes, give or take."

"Cool! I can get myself ready in time, especially since I don't need to put on any makeup or comb my hair." I started to rise from the bed, and he came out of the bathroom.

"I don't think so," he said. "You need to stay home and rest."

Barney was never one to tell me "No." He never had to in the past. He knew me, and he accepted that if I said I was going to do something, there was no stopping me. That's just the way I was. But now I was harming myself, he knew it, and he wasn't going to allow it.

My mind screamed silently, *I am done with the treatments!* My body, though, agreed with my husband. Without a word, I lay back down and was instantly asleep. When I woke up, I looked at the clock by the bed. It was 11:00 a.m. Worship was probably just underway. Depression drenched me. *I want to be in church so bad!* I then hosted my own pity party, complete with hor d'oeuvres and little finger sandwiches, until I decided to make a phone call. For reasons I don't quite know, I called my friend Gloria in California. She was at church herself and had just finished her Sunday school class. "Hey, Jac. What's up?"

"I'm so tired of not feeling good," I whined through the wrenching sobs of my ugly cry. "My neck is killing me. I just want to go to church."

"It's okay. You can break down and have a fit," Gloria conceded. "Just don't stay there." She then prayed for me, and I was weeping by the time she said her Amen. "It's funny you're calling right now," she then said, "because Bill has declared today 'Barney and Jacki Day' here at the church." I wasn't sure I heard her correctly. They lived in Sacramento. We'd never been members of their church. "Bill said we took up an offering for you guys." They certainly had, to the tune of one thousand dollars, a fortune considering it was from a small congregation.

When Barney got home, I told him all about my call to Gloria and "Barney and Jacki Day," but left out the pity party part. It's not like there were any hor d'oeuvres left, anyway.

Then Monday came and my obstinate streak returned. Aja, who was by then in the final days of her pregnancy with Alijah, stopped by the house on the way to Target. "I'm going with you,"

Why it is important to transition from sorrow to joy

A crown of beauty instead of ashes,
the oil of joy instead of mourning, and a garment
of praise instead of a spirit of despair. —Isaiah 61:3

The passage found in Isaiah paints a contrasting picture. Ashes placed on the head were a traditional symbol of mourning, either for a death or a tragic circumstance. Oil was used, especially by women, as a body ointment; the lack of oil was also a sign of mourning. Despair is an emotion easily associated with mourning. Yet in the midst of all of this hopelessness, it is possible to experience God's renewal, bearing witness to the world of the graciousness of the Lord.

Sadness and grief are inevitable. They can literally take you to your knees. I've learned that I can lift my head to the Lord and receive the comfort that only He gives. Sometimes it feels as though wallowing in my sorrow is easier than turning to the Lord. So I must make a conscious decision to allow God to minister to me. It doesn't mean that the source of my sadness is eliminated, but there's the testimony—I express joy and praise out of the pain!

Transition from sorrow to joy and be a channel from God to the hurting, oppressed, and hopeless people around you.

I said, once more defying my body's call for retreat—and common sense. But this wasn't like my foolishness on Saturday. She was driving and I wasn't alone, right? We walked inside to get our carts, and the same wooziness hit me with a vengeance. I knew I was in trouble. Plus, this was Aja, my emotional one. If I passed out on her, she'd go into labor right then and there!

"I'm not feeling good," I said, trying to understate the severity of my weakness. "Can you take me back to the car?" She not only did that; she took me home. Bo came over and sat with me, and Aja called Barney to tell him what had happened. When he got home, he didn't say anything. He didn't have to. I could tell he was fuming. I could only imagine what he was thinking. *You're sick. Your daughter is pregnant. Did you ever think about what might've happened?* The silent treatment continued all the way up until bedtime—the time when we had started our now-beloved "How's your day" routine.

Barney looked at me. His eyes were like simmering coals. "Are you trying to kill yourself?"

That wasn't what I was expecting to hear. I got my sassy attitude on. "What are you talking about?"

"You didn't need to go to Target. What were you thinking?"

Look, dude! I'm the one that has cancer. I'm the one that has gone through hell for the last four months. Maybe I shouldn't have gone, but I just wanted to get out of this house and do something normal!

That's what I thought, not what I said. When we were under the covers, I finally responded. "No," I said. "I'm not trying to kill myself. Everybody has gone through this with me. You have. But no one has felt what I've felt, or endured what I've endured. I just wanted a little bit of normal. That's why I went." Then I added, "Tomorrow I won't go. But a few days later, I just might."

I glared at him, and he had a blank stare that told me he was processing everything I'd said, analyzing it, and measuring his response. He finally spoke. "Would you please be careful?"

I'll be careful, I thought. *But I'm not gonna stay stuck in this house.*

I appreciated my stubbornness, in that I felt it was serving to strengthen my resolve. But my headstrong attitude did nothing to prepare me for what was coming next.

My real torture was about to begin.

Chapter Four

The church was packed with glowing faces from whom light seemed to project from within, filling the atmosphere with streaming beams of God's presence. The ethereal space around me was teaming with praise to the Lord. I could practically see the harmonies and voices rising to Heaven like the smoke of burning incense. As I looked to my left and then to my right, my precious brothers and sisters returned my glance, eyes beaming with anticipation of the day I would confirm my healing to them. I arched my head toward the sky and peered beyond the ceiling into the heavenly realms themselves, seeing the very angels of God dancing in joy.

Then a slate grey cloud zoomed in, sudden and cold, blocking my view. The music of worship faded to a muted din, minor chords changing to major, clanging against my consciousness like a perverse tune from a creepy carousel. Then, just as quickly, silence descended. I still saw the inside of the church, but everything was in slow motion, twisted and distorted.

And then the voice came, as it had every other time before. Cynical. Sinister. Accusing.

"What are you going to say to people when the cancer's not gone?" it mocked. "What is that going to do to your so-called testimony? What are you going to do then?"

Sometimes I jolted straight up in the bed. Other times I simply woke up, watched the familiar surroundings of my bedroom swim into reality, and then cry—not the ugly one, but something even more pathetic, laced with tears of defeat and despair.

The same nightmare came and returned about every other night during the first six weeks of my eight-week wait for the results of my treatments, planting and watering a seed of doubt that I never anticipated. Satan had planned well. All through the chemotherapy and radiation, all amidst the weakness and the sickness, I knew I was going to be healed. My commitment was unwavering. I was eager to share my anticipated victorious outcome to anyone who'd listen. Then, immediately after my weekend of willful pigheadedness, the dreams began. I knew what they were. I understood the devil had declared spiritual war on my heart and mind. The accuser was accusing—it's what he does.

But I'd never been in this kind of battle. I'd always heard the old saints say, "If the devil is after you, it's because God has *big* plans for you. He wants you to stop what you're doing for God." I remembered that testimony, but I still wasn't ready for the severity of the attacks. They were constant, and remembrances of the nightmare during the day would accentuate the diabolical dialogue: "What are you going to do then?" Another query pressed in, but it was my voice that was speaking. *Are you going to want to go through it again?* The first time around, I had no idea what the cancer treatments were going to be like, and I didn't feel like I had a choice about it anyway. Now that I had experienced the treatments and their aftermath, I really wasn't sure if I wanted to do it a second time around—or even if I could do it at all.

It was torture, delivered straight from the very pit of Hell.

And it was a battle I had to wage alone. After all, I was the one God had spoken to about the outcome of all of this: "It's not

How to be ready for the enemy's unexpected attacks

Put on the full armor of God so that you can take your stand against the devil's schemes. —Ephesians 6:11

Technically, none of the enemy's attacks should be unexpected. It's what he does! But we definitely get caught off guard at times. I was "breezing through" my cancer journey with the assurance that God was going to heal me. I looked at the months of treatments and everything they entailed as part of the process. I was so confident in God's promise, I forgot there was another player in the process. Satan. He did what he does best. Torture and torment.

Paul instructs us in Ephesians on how to combat the enemy. No soldier goes into battle unprepared. They leave civilian life and spend weeks in Boot Camp training mentally, physically, and strategically to go to war. Everything changes, even their clothing—all in preparation for the fight in which they will engage.

The "full armor" means "complete" armor, both offensive and defensive, so that we can stand against the schemes of the enemy. He doesn't fight fair! Satan does not carry on an open warfare. He does not meet the Christian soldier face to face. His advances are skillful, cunning attempts conducted in darkness. Do not be caught unprepared for the attack of Satan. Put on the whole armor of God!

about you, Jacki." But it was. Not that I would take the glory for any of it. But it was a test of *my* faith and obedience. So many people had prayed, fasted, and walked alongside me on this journey, yet I discerned this was a "rubber meets the road" moment. It was up to me to fight the battle and I didn't want any casualties. Satan couldn't attack my friends or loved ones because of me. So I never told Barney, or the girls, or Bo and Diana, or anyone else. I didn't even share it with my PIT Crew. I knew it had to be just Satan and me—gloves off, standing toe-to-toe in the middle of the squared circle, trading blows until the end. Winner takes all, even if it meant my life.

During this conflict, I felt a constant weight on my shoulders, as real as if I had a noose around my neck with an anchor at the end of the rope. I could tell others sensed something was wrong, but they simply assumed I still wasn't feeling well physically. That wasn't it; my body was strengthening with each day. But I was carrying a burden. Satan wouldn't let go, but hung on for all he was worth. Then, at the close of the sixth week, came the Sunday that our pastor's wife, Karen, was scheduled to speak at another church. Barney and I joined a group from our congregation that accompanied her to hear her message. I don't recall anything she said, though, because the voice of the accuser came along, too. He said the same things in the same place and in the same way he had in the dreams. Satan was bold; he was taunting me right there in the house of God! My nightmares had become reality.

Normally an altar call was given at the close of services, but that night First Lady Karen did something quite unusual. She asked people to stand up and testify if they had been inspired by something she had said during the sermon. Again, I didn't remember a word she said, but I did hear God's Spirit break through the mumblings of the voice and tell me to rise to my feet. *Jacki, you need to put your foot on the devil's neck. It's time to shut him up! Know that I am God!* I opened my mouth to speak and told them everything, my ugly cry in full form. But I didn't care. It had to be said. "I don't know what's going to happen in the next couple of weeks," I concluded, "but I'm declaring that I am healed! I'm no longer going to be tortured by the enemy!"

Knockout.

The weight was gone. The nightmares ceased. The voice shut up. It never returned.

The next two weeks, I continued feeling stronger physically and had absolute certainty that I was healed. It was just a matter of hearing the confirmation. In the meantime, I received a letter from my friends Sandra and Steve in California in response to a phone conversation I had with Sandra when I was feeling a little down. It contained a check and was dated April 2. It affirmed God's presence and provision, and my victory over Satan. It read:

Hello Brother and Sissy,

I am especially happy to write this note and very grateful that God would use me in His plan for you! Here are the rules:

$250 for Jacki – can only be spent on Jacki

$250 for Barney – can only be spent on Barney, unless of course you decide to spend some on Jacki

$250 for other stuff—house, car, groceries—and every dime has to be spent in the Murray household

This is a gift from our hearts to yours. We look forward to seeing you as soon as the Lord allows.

Love and friendship,

Sandra and Steve

On the morning of April 15, I rose out of bed and couldn't wait to get to the clinic for the PET scan. Upon arrival, I was given a double dose of my Xanax. Next, I was called back into a triage room and received an injection of dye in my arm. The lights were dimmed to help me relax and to allow the Xanax to do its work. About thirty minutes later, I was taken into the room with the MRI machine, lay down on the platform, and was slid headfirst into the tube. I closed my eyes the entire time, knowing the top of the tube was an inch away from the tip of my nose. It was definitely snug. Yet I was remarkably calm, in part because of the Xanax but also because of my comforting assurance from the Lord. *This is just another part of the process*, I thought, *another point in the testimony. I am healed!* I even dozed off during the forty-five minute procedure.

> On the morning of April 15, I couldn't wait to get to the clinic.

Afterward, still groggy from the experience, Barney drove me home. Later that afternoon, I received confirmation from Aryn in Phoenix that she had given birth to our third grandson, Ajani. It was her second child, and Aryn's labor was once again induced because she has a rare liver disease that, when pregnant, causes a secondary condition that can cause stillbirth. Nevertheless, both mother and child were healthy. Paired with the birth of baby Alijah to Aja (her second boy) on March 12, I was doubly blessed. Three days later I was due to get the results of the PET scan. I wasn't fretful or even overly anticipatory. I slept well, resting in the confidence that can only come from the Lord.

Barney and I arrived at Dr. Manning's office the morning of April 18. We were called back into one of his exam rooms and saw his nursing assistant. She had tears in her eyes. "Your report," she said, "is fabulous!" She probably wasn't supposed to give anything away, but I guess she couldn't help herself. I just smiled as we were directed to our room. Moments later, Dr. Manning came in and sat down on the stool. He wheeled himself closer.

"Take a look at this," he said, holding up my chart, "and read what it says."

I told him I couldn't read it because I didn't have my glasses. "You tell me what it says," I directed.

He started reading and rattled off quite a bit of medical jargon before getting to the final four words. He grinned from ear to ear, far more personable than he was during my first visit with him.

"No trace of cancer."

I always thought that when I finally heard those words, I would leap to my feet, shout to the Lord, and probably even do a little happy dance. But it wasn't anything like that at all. Instead, I sat there and responded from a place of holy reverence and confidence that was deeper than mere emotion.

I smiled. "I knew I was going to be healed," I said.

Barney sat there looking at his phone. He didn't even raise his head. Our assurance from God was *that* undeniable. Dr. Manning wasn't sure what to do with our seemingly muted responses, but he recognized the significance of the diagnosis. Sort of. "You're my miracle," he stated. I looked at him. "I am a miracle," I clarified, "but I'm not your miracle." He wasn't offended. He knew exactly what I was saying. Today, he refers to me as his "poster child."

From the very beginning when God told me, "This isn't about you, Jacki. This is about the testimony that is going to come out of it. I will get the glory," I believed I was going to be healed. I did my best to live that way—leading up to the chemotherapy, through those treatments and into the radiation, and then beyond when Satan himself warred against my very soul—and I saw it all as a process that I would navigate in God's timing and in His way.

Now the day had come. I had arrived! I was healed!

We drove home and then I headed over to Bo's house. She was there with her sister Sandra. I looked at my friend. "I am cancer free!" Bo teared up and gave me a kiss, and Sandra took a photo to capture the moment. Then I walked over to Diana's. She was with a client, but when I walked in the entrance to the salon, Diana stopped and looked up from the table. "Well?" she asked. I responded, "I'm cancer free!" And then, utterly unexpected, I started crying. Diana came over and embraced me, the first time she ever gave me a hug, and her client congratulated me. It was wonderful!

I returned to the house and called Mommy. Her response was classic. "Well, you always got what you wanted." She was happy, of course, and announced that she couldn't wait to share my testimony with the saints in Florida. Though she didn't say it specifically, I can only imagine the utter joy she felt about not losing another child. I don't think she would've been able to endure that. Next I called Aja to give her the news. I told her I was cancer free and, unlike the day I told her I had cancer, there was no emotional outburst, no falling apart. "Wow Mom! Cool beans!" she said. She'd been with me in person through so much of the past five months, and witnessed how I was living out my faith, and her reaction reflected that. Then I got ready to call Aryn. I thought about her and the past five months. When I was first diagnosed, we stayed in touch with each other, but after a while she stopped calling regularly and, when she did, we didn't discuss the cancer. She was going through her pregnancy then, and I knew she was concerned about her baby's safety because

How to have His perspective in your season of pain

There is a time for everything, and a season for every activity under the heavens. —Ecclesiastes 3:1

Timing is everything. Solomon tells us here that all of life is really a matter of timing. God has a plan for everyone's life and it is critical to live with an awareness of His timing for you. We all go through cycles, each with its own purpose. Sometimes we face problems that seem to go against God's plan. Yet the events of our lives do not randomly happen by chance; God has a reason.

I never imagined that I would have cancer, especially a rare head and neck cancer. But from the beginning of time, God knew. There was a purpose even in cancer. That purpose or reason was so much bigger than me. I had to go through it, when and how I did, to fulfill God's plan for my life.

Is it possible to honor, love, and worship God in difficult seasons? Is it possible to find joy in the midst of your sickness and depend on Him even in failing health? Is it possible to remain close to God when He doesn't seem close at all? Yes! If you only thank God in seasons of good health and prosperity, you are missing true worship.

The most difficult of situations can remind us that without God, life's problems have no lasting solutions. Rely on God, no matter what—and you'll find joy in the midst of each season and in all of the transitions in between.

of her liver ailment. Her disassociation during my cancer treatments didn't hurt my feelings, but it did surprise me a bit. As I pushed auto dial, I wondered how she was going to react.

"Hey Aryn," I said, "I'm cancer free!"

She paused, but I was sure I heard an audible breath of relief. "That's great news, Ma!" And then we immediately launched into small talk about our visit the next day to see baby Ajani. It was all very matter-of-fact—and very much like Aryn; not a lot of emotion, but I knew she was happy. That night Barney went to church for a Bible study and told our pastor, Sean Bailey, the good news. He was overjoyed and requested that I share my story and diagnosis with the congregation the following Sunday.

The next morning, it was time to head up to Phoenix and see baby Ajani. It's a trek Barney and I had made so many times before, and there's not much to see along the one hundred mile-plus stretch of desert between Tucson and Phoenix. We were our typical selves: quiet (Barney calls driving his "thinking time") and reflective. But considering the news of the previous day, this drive *was* different. I liken it to holding a Mickey Mouse balloon within a larger oval balloon. The smaller balloon with the ears inside was the normalcy of the moment, riding on the freeway like always, but everything was surrounded by this outer balloon that screamed, "You just beat cancer—and you're now going to see your number four grandchild for the first time!" As we went through the last mountain pass and started down the hill toward the southern outskirts of Phoenix, Barney finally spoke.

> "Well, baby, praise God!"

"Well, baby, praise God!"

I couldn't have said it better myself.

Chapter Five

We had a blast at Aryn's house. Aja and Glenn drove up from Tucson as well, so it was the first time all four grandchildren were together. Two-year-old Arilàn, Ajani's big sister, didn't take it well. She was the only girl, and it was clear she wasn't pleased with her brother and cousins. Barney took a bunch of pictures, and in every one of them Arilàn is looking the other way, arms crossed and with a scowl on her face. Pure attitude. I don't know where she gets it from. It wasn't until after the boys were away playing that Arilàn smiled for the first time. She did it for a picture while alone in my lap. The coolest thing about the trip was that it wasn't about me being cancer-free. It was all about the grandbabies, and that's exactly the way I wanted it.

We stayed the night and drove home the next morning—which just happened to be our twenty-eighth wedding anniversary. With everything that had happened over the past few days, we didn't do anything in particular to celebrate. That's okay. That night, sitting on the sofa, I looked over at Barney and whispered a prayer of gratitude to God. There he was, that same little boy that was standing on a chair next to my high chair for my first birthday fifty years later. Present. Consistent. Constant.

One week later, it was time to share my testimony at church. Pastor Bailey, a large man with a Jamaican accent, was so excited as he introduced me. Because we joined the church just after I was diagnosed, many of the people in the congregation knew of me, but they didn't know much of my story. I briefly filled in the details from the previous five months, and then told them the happy news of my healing.

"Here I am today," I concluded. "I knew He was going to do it, and now He has. God really did it!"

With that declaration, something broke loose within me. I started singing "His Eye is on the Sparrow," the same song I performed months earlier for Pastor Horace Sheppard, but I couldn't get through it. I motioned to the choir director, and as she took the microphone and finished the song, I did my happy dance. I was crying, praising, and doing a jig! Through the dynamic of giving my testimony, the physical manifestation of utter joy just poured forth from me. Before I knew it, the other church members—most of whom I barely knew but who had persistently prayed for me—started cutting a rug with me! The entire house was blessed!

> "God really did it!"

We had ourselves a time. We sure did.

After learning I was cancer-free, I knew it was time to send a significant message to some very significant people. I went to my computer, opened up my email, and started typing.

Hello Everyone,

It's been a few weeks since I last emailed. Recovery from radiation treatments is going well. I feel a little better every day. Still dealing with some of the side effects, but they are coming along.

I wanted to share something with all of you. It's my

way of saying thank you. I'm sure you remember when I sent the email requesting that you be my "Personal Intercessory Team." Barney calls you my PIT Crew. One of the things that upset me most when I was first diagnosed was that I felt I would have to go through this alone, without any of my friends and sisters near me to help me go through. The Lord quickly let me know that I was not alone, and you were the specific people He gave me to ask to pray specifically. I knew I could share all the details of the disease and what I was feeling with you and you would PRAY. I knew I could trust you with my heart—something that's not very easy for me to do.

Now that I'm finished treatments and feeling so much better, I wanted to say thank you—

for all your prayers

for your love and support

for the many cards, flowers and gifts

for all your prayers

for the daily, weekly, bi-weekly, monthly phone calls

for the financial blessings (they always came right on time!)

for all your prayers

for taking the time out of your schedules for me

for the fasts that were done on my behalf

for all your prayers

for taking the time and expense to come to visit

for all your prayers

Please click on the link below (turn up your volume) and it will finish what I want to say. I love you.

The link was to a video slide show Barney put together and posted on YouTube. It had photos of me taken through the course of my cancer with an inspirational song by Marvin Sapp playing in the background—and it let viewers know that I was cancer-free. Reactions, of course, were joyful and heartfelt. Carolynn's teenage son Donovan watched the slide show as she watched it. He was aware of the cancer, but did not realize how bad it had been until he saw the video. She said he broke down in tears.

The sending of the video and the giving of the testimony at church marked the beginning of a new season in my life. I went back to work in church, but not nearly as actively as I used to in California. I became leader of the worship team. Barney and I worked on song lists, and then I taught the team those songs at our rehearsals every Saturday morning. Of course, I sang with the team as well, and my hearing and my voice were fully restored. Worship was a pleasure that I appreciated more than ever before. I also started working with the church's women's ministry, assisting First Lady Karen with a Bible study every Tuesday morning. But that was it. During the time I had cancer, I recognized how burned out I'd become in California, and I now understood that while I was feeling better after the cancer, I wasn't one hundred percent and needed to embrace and maintain a lighter responsibility load at church.

I also recognized that being cancer free wasn't the end of the story. Sometime along the journey God told me that my story was going to be told to "numbers unknown." In a vision, He showed me standing in a large convention center-type auditorium speaking to thousands of people. I knew He was going to use my story to encourage His people, so I had to remain available to Him. My life focus was no longer to be about "church work" but more on "Kingdom work."

Not long after I was cancer-free, I also realized something else that was remarkable—my diabetes had vanished. Perhaps it was the result of losing all of that weight, or maybe God decided to include the defeat of diabetes in my supernatural healing. Likely, it was a bit of both, but all I knew was that I didn't need to take the metformin pills any longer, the blood sugar was stable, and each subsequent visit to my primary care doctor confirmed my good health. My body corrected itself with the help of the Lord.

In the months to come, the routine of life returned and was, well, delightfully routine. Aja went back to work, so I took care of Aren and Alijah for a while until Aja and Glenn ultimately moved up to Phoenix because of his job and to be closer to Aryn and her family. I got back to cooking meals, including my beloved homemade ice cream, and taking care of the household chores. The stomach tube was removed in June, but by then I was already eating normally once again. On Memorial Day, Mommy, Lori, and Germaine came into town for a visit. True to form, I had to reassure Mommy that there wasn't a dire reason for the visit; she was convinced I was going to announce that the cancer had returned and that I had only six months to live. In July, Barney and I drove to our old stomping grounds in California to visit friends. I was asked to give my testimony at Maranatha Christian Center and was also allowed to sing "God is Standing By" with the choir. Both Thanksgiving and Christmas were wonderful; I ate what I wanted, within reasonable limits, and put up decorations like a storm. Sitting on the sofa one afternoon looking at the tree with Bo, I couldn't believe it was only one year earlier that I was in the throes of the cancer treatments.

It was cool to be healed. God is so awesome!

> *Being cancer free wasn't the end of the story.*

On September 12, 2009, The King's Daughters Dance Ministry, under the leadership of Apostle Joyce Stevens and the direction of Janet Chacon, presented the Anointed Soles Dance Show entitled, "Never Would Have Made It" at the Berger Performing Arts Center in Tucson. Janet had been my hair stylist since our move to Tucson and knew about my journey. The dance show was dedicated to "the Lord God Almighty, to acknowledge His gifts of mercy and healing" in my life. The performance featured sixteen dance pieces choreographed to music by Kirk Franklin, Israel Houghton, Donnie McClurkin, and other gifted artists. On the opening page of the program, Barney wrote a piece he titled, "One Good Thing." It reads:

Proverbs 18:22 says, "He who finds a wife finds a good thing, and obtains favor from the Lord." My good thing is Jacki Murray. Having grown up together and being married for the last twenty-nine years, we found ourselves challenged by the economy but took pleasure in what God had blessed us with: His promises and the power of His love toward us. The joy of spending time with our children and four grandchildren kept us grounded and our priorities in order.

All of this came under test when we found out from Jacki's doctor that what was believed to be an infection was actually Stage Four head and neck cancer. How did this African American woman get a rare cancer usually found in Asia, predominately in men that smoke excessively? That was the natural question. "Lord, what is it you want me to get out of this?" Jacki asked. The Lord gave Jacki peace in knowing that this has to be a supernatural healing so that everyone will know it was God. Jacki gets the testimony, but God gets the glory out of it.

As we trusted the Lord through weeks of chemotherapy, followed by weeks of the maximum radiation allowed, Jacki's purpose became more of a reality. In her suffering, Jacki kept a journal of her experiences and has started writing a book. This experience is not about Jacki but about those she will meet and the difference her testimony will make in their lives.

Coming up now on two years since Jacki started treatments, healing has taken place and restoration is in progress. Medical follow-up cannot find any issues. None. Today she stands before you victorious through the blood of Jesus, a symbol of what God can do when you trust Him and purpose to live within His will.

I thank God for what He has done and brought us through. As a husband, father, and man of God, I thank Him for His strength and encouragement to stay in place, stand tall, and watch Him show Himself true to His Word. Most of all, thank you, Lord, for my "good thing."

Barney and Jacki, January 1957
Where the love story begins…she was one, he was two.

Gene, Jacki, and Daryl, 1959
Family photo with Jacki and her sibling brothers.

Jacki with Baby Aren, Aja, Aryn, Lori, Mommy with Baby Arilàn
Four generations of the Hughes Family.

Germaine (Cuz), Martha (Auntie), Aryn
Thanksgiving 2007. Thank God for the cooks!

Jacki's sister, Lori, and Baby Aren
Thanksgiving 2007. Thankful for family.

Family Photo
Thanksgiving 2007.
Nothing like family!

Christmas 2007 at Aryn and Delawn's house in Phoenix
The babies opening their gifts;
more like playing with the wrapping paper!

Your strength may
surprise you.

An encouraging card from Margaret,
my "radiation buddy" at Arizona Oncology

Arilàn and Nana
Sharing a special moment. She had no idea
she was touching one of the tumors.

Barney and Jacki's Birthday Party, January 2008
Happy Birthday Jacki and Barney!

Jacki and Barney
Blowing out the candles…50 years after their first party together!

Aja and Aryn (Birthday Party)
Say cheese! Happy Birthday Mom and Dad!

Glenn (Birthday Party)
They had afros back in the 80's?

Delawn (Birthday Party)
Cool dude!

Aren (Birthday Party)
What's Disco?

Arilàn (Birthday Party)
Afro puff girl!

Jacki and Janice (Birthday Party)
Special friends…We remember the 80's!

Lisa and Davita (Birthday Party)
All the way from Atlanta and Boston!

Della, Jacki, and the boys
(Birthday Party)
She drove all the way
from California by herself.
My friends *are* family!

Bo, Jacki, and Doug (Birthday Party)
Let's get this party started!

Bo's gift. Time is precious!

After my chemo treatments were done, Aja treated me to a makeover at the Mac counter at Dillards.

Papa, Nana, and Aren
Aren seemed to not mind Nana's bald head. This was his way of "kissing" Nana.

Alyse Calhoun
She shaved all of her
hair off in honor of
Auntie Jacki.

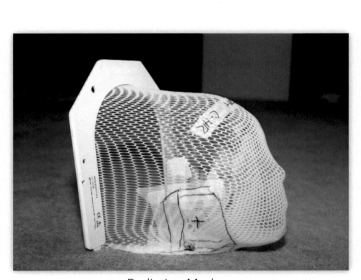

Radiation Mask
It's still eerie seeing this!
The markings show how the tumor was shrinking.

Nana with Baby Ajani, April 2008
First time holding Ajani. Double blessing!

Nana with Baby Alijah,
March 2008
First time holding Alijah
right after birth.
What a blessing!

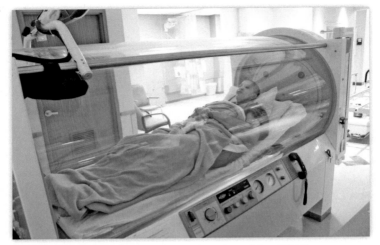

Hyperbaric oxygen chamber, May 2015
Two hours per day, five days per week, for four weeks. Yikes!

Aryn, Barney, Jacki, Ajani,
and Arilàn, January 2015
Family photo at Papa's 60th
birthday dinner

Clara Belle and Jacki, Christmas
with the Murrays, 2007

Glenn and Aja

The Williamson Kids, Easter 2015
Lauren, Aizak Hilton, Aren, Alijah, and Asè

Bo with a kiss for Jacki when
she learned Jacki was cancer free!

Jacki, January 2007; Before it all began…

Jacki, September 2015
Thank you Lord
for your grace!

Chapter Six

June 2015

Over seven years since being diagnosed cancer free

I no longer have cancer, but cancer will always be with me.

It's part of my story. The whole experience has helped make me who I am now. I never say that I'm in remission. I always say that I'm healed. But cancer will always be with me.

I deal with many side effects from the treatments. Because the radiation was administered to my head and neck, I lost use of my salivary glands. Nobody thinks about their spit. When you get dry, you swallow. When you take a bite of food, you swallow. If I were to take a bite of bread without water, I'd keep chewing and never be able to swallow. Water is my drink of choice not because it's healthy, but because it's necessary. This side effect has also caused dental issues such as my teeth falling out. As I write this, oral surgery is ahead, and to prepare I've had to spend thirty weekly sessions inside a hyperbaric oxygen chamber because blood is not properly flowing to my gums. Let's just say that chamber, though transparent, is just as uncomfortably cozy as an MRI tube. I had a throat infection a couple of years ago that normally would've been minor, but I ended up in the hospital for twenty-two days and even needed a blood transfusion. I've had shingles on my face where the radiation was done. Chicken pox itches, but shingles hurt. The swelling was so bad I looked like a prizefighter that ended up on the wrong end of a barrage of punches from Mike Tyson. My face was a blistered boil, and there was even danger of blindness because the shingles were so close to my eyes.

None of these side effects are fun, and they're certainly not easy, but they're the best things that have ever happened to me because they're a reminder of how God has healed me of cancer and kept His promise. God never, ever goes back on His word. Had I not had cancer, these new conditions would've been more challenging. Now I see them as yet another opportunity to declare to others what God has done—and continues to do—in my life. These side effects are also a reminder of how skillfully God has created our bodies. We are intricately designed.

> God loves us.
> We are fearfully and
> wonderfully made!

Every cell, every muscle, every organ, every aspect of our bodies has purpose. It confirms to me how much God loves us. We are fearfully and wonderfully made!

Even as I finalized my work on this book, I developed blood pressure and heart issues. One Sunday I had to leave church and go to the ER because my blood pressure spiked. But again I'm reminded, "If God can handle cancer, He can handle this." Sure, it's scary at times, but in the Bible Paul tells us God has not given us a spirit of fear, but of power, love, and a sound mind.

Many wonderful things have happened since being cancer free. One special moment came on the first anniversary of the news. It was a Sunday and I decided I needed to be in church even though, at the time, Barney and I did not have a church home. I visited a church not far from our home, New Destiny

Church International, and Barney decided he was going to stay home. The congregation was small but warm and welcoming. When the message was finished, the pastor opened up the altar for prayer, and I went forward simply to thank God for my healing. A woman came up behind me to pray with me. I'd never met her before, but the touch of her hand on the back of my shoulder was comforting and felt somehow familiar. It was almost as though God was saying to me, "I know you're thankful. I know you're grateful. I know, my daughter, I know," and I was so overcome with His peaceful presence that I began crying. The tears were cleansing. I recalled the hours of chemotherapy, weeks of radiation, and everything that happened during those months of treatment and the recovery period afterward. It was overwhelming. After the time of prayer, the pastor asked if anyone had anything to say, and I shared a part of my testimony and expressed my thankfulness to God.

When the service was dismissed, the woman who prayed with me came over to introduce herself. Her name was JoAnne Ware, and I learned that she was a fellow New Yorker, giving us an immediate connection. Over a year later, I saw JoAnne again; Barney and I were guest speakers at a couple's retreat in Phoenix, and she and her husband Sean were in attendance. Again, it was as though we had been friends for years. Today, JoAnne remains a special person in my life. We call each other "Fam" (short for "family") and have shared many occasions with her, Sean, and their three children. She frequently calls me when she's frustrated and needs someone, as she puts it, to "talk her off the edge." She's one of the few people with whom I can truly be myself with no fear of judgment. She loves me unconditionally. I am forever grateful the Lord allowed our paths to cross at that church altar. I have no doubt that it was a divine appointment.

Cancer will always be with me, too, because it has changed me in ways I otherwise would not have experienced. It has deepened my relationship with God; until the diagnosis, I never had to suffer. I always had a Plan B. I always had an answer. I always had Barney to rescue me. With cancer, I really had to learn to *trust* God. It was my opportunity to walk it out and live it out—and through Him, I lived *Cancer With Grace*. Thanks to the cancer, I finally saw for myself the God that I remembered seeing as a little girl being preached about in tent revivals and doing works of deliverance. His healing was no longer something I heard about; it was something I experienced.

Now, God has privileged me to speak to people at worship events, conferences, and one-on-one—and every time I say the same thing. Don't make a big deal out of the fact I had cancer. Yes, it's glorious that our God can overcome such a deadly disease, and I'm here today because He did just that. But while it was cancer for me, for you it might be an unexpected financial situation, a devastating relationship issue, or a circumstance that has challenged your faith to its very core. Whatever it is, it may not be the same issue as mine—but He's definitely the same God. The faith I have is no different than the faith you possess. Faith is faith, and God is the same yesterday, today, and forever.

He is a God of His word. He gave me a promise, and He delivered on that promise. He'll do the same for you as you receive His promise and believe in it. Everything He said in His promise still abides—right now. Trust in Him! You will not be disappointed, and you will be given your own testimony of His grace, to His praise and glory.

Chapter Seven

Cancer With Grace: A Husband's Perspective
by Barney Hilton Murray

My father was the strong, silent type, not the least bit emotional, and he kept his distance but remained busy behind the scenes. If I wanted to spend time with him, I worked at his side, learning auto body repair while working on cars. This is where I learned what it meant to have a strong work ethic. There was never a question about whether or not my father loved me—I knew that he did, and I also understood that he knew how to take care of his family and would do anything for us.

Still, I purposed in my heart that what he didn't give me in terms of time and affection I would give to my family. I was determined to be the dad who was there in the bleachers; it wasn't enough to only congratulate the kids when they got home.

So I certainly wasn't going to stand on the sidelines for my wife when we were told she had cancer. It wasn't in my DNA. Besides, the ongoing stability of my home was my responsibility. One that I took, as it turned out, more seriously than I thought.

Looking back, those months of diagnosis, testing, chemotherapy, radiation, and recovery are a blur because of the mindset I had to maintain. I didn't have the luxury of entertaining thoughts that distracted me from what I needed to do. Like the ringside bell that clangs for the boxer, I acted by reflex, responding when called upon. Yes, I had fear and anxiety that I could lose my wife—and even today, those feelings of despair can come and go. Cancer will always be a part of me, too. Much like the bell, it resonates. But knowing that God said she was going to be healed, those months turned into a journey with some significant stops for me along the way—and it was a journey void of shortcuts. The healing was coming on the back end. It was the final exam. It was as though God was saying, "You're going to ace this test, but you're still going to have to take it."

> I acted by reflex, responding when called upon.

One vital stop along the way came in realizing how locked in I became once we were underway. I had to juggle many parts and finesse many people to make sure Jacki was as comfortable as possible. My methodical, analytical nature served me well and kept me from wavering. In truth, I became "spiritually suicidal" in my commitment. Because God had spoken, it didn't need to make any sense to me, and no explanation was required. I'd seen and experienced too much in my relationship with Him to take my eye off the target. His word was all I needed. This was my time for blind obedience.

As a result, when Jacki was down, I was up. It's a dynamic that has played itself out in our marriage time and again. You won't find both of us down at the same time. I suppose that's why I told her, "It's going to be okay" when she said "I don't want to do this" the morning after her visit to a skeptical Dr. Manning after diagnosis. I believe anything shared is either twice as good or half as bad. If you can have somebody to walk through it with you, it's only half as bad because they're sharing some of the burden; when things are well, it's twice as good because you're not alone.

Another pivotal stop in my journey of *Cancer With Grace* came right after Jacki started her radiation treatments. I was unemployed at the time, and out of necessity, knew my career needed to be reengineered. I enrolled at a local community college and took courses in graphic design and photojournalism. In the latter class, we were given an assignment to interview and write an article about one of our classmates. A lady about my age was designated to interview me, and we starting talking about our families. I described Jacki's cancer treatments and her determination, and mentioned how I was responding to her illness as her husband. About three-fourths of the way through the interview, the woman paused. She asked an unexpected question.

"Why are you doing this?"

I wasn't sure I'd heard her correctly. "Huh?"

"I mean, you're dealing with a lot of stuff, and you're in school, and your wife is sick. Why are you still there?"

My response was direct and unrehearsed. "I have no other choice."

For the next twenty minutes, we debated. "Why do you feel you don't have a choice? Everyone has a choice," she insisted.

I tried to explain the beliefs that were foundational to my core values as a husband—as a man—as a Christian. "I did not sign up for what was being manifested," I said, referring to the cancer, "but I did say 'til death do us part' in my vows, and those vows mean something. I must be true to my word. So I don't have a choice."

By the time class ended, we went our separate ways. "I have to write the story," she said, "but I want you to know you still have a choice." I just shook my head. She still didn't get it.

But I did get it—in a greater way than ever before. As I drove home, I realized that interview had put me on the spot. It made me articulate my battle. The battle was not with cancer or with Jacki. The battle was with Barney the man. *Am I really who I believe that I am? Am I real or not?* It was a defining moment. Her question challenged my mindset and served to clarify it. My integrity and my love for Jacki, my kids, and for each person in the community was why I was doing what I was doing. It was undeniably "a God thing" for me.

It was not surprising, then, that a final stop in the journey for me was the increased intimacy I experienced with Jacki in our late night conversations. The God-given gift of being an entrepreneur is to be in service to others. He has blessed me with several gifts and tools to meet the needs of His people. It's part of my nature, so my mind is always going, always thinking. I often say I want to wear out, not rust out. But the cancer brought things down to what was really important. Jacki became the most important "client" I had. She required my time and energy. She needed me to be physically there and emotionally engaged. It became all about us being one; all we had was each other. This was our journey and test. There were a lot of spectators in the stands, but we were the only ones on the field. We needed to stick together—and stick close.

> We needed to stick together— and stick close.

Admittedly, seven years later, we're trying to get back to that place of intimacy once again. I'm confident, though, that we're going to make it.

Finally, one of the most vivid images I can remember from Jacki's time with cancer was being in the bathroom while she showered, holding her chemo pump and sitting on the edge of the toilet so I could be there to help her if she fell. I was on edge, expecting the worst and praying for the best. It was that way every day. I was at peak level and peak sensitivity. I didn't have the privilege of worrying about me. It was always us. Everything was going out; nothing was coming in. I've heard it said that the hardest part about being strong is no one asks how you're doing. One of the demons that I still deal with now as I look back and process it all is wondering, "With all that I sacrificed, when is it my turn? When can I feel that level of support that Jacki felt?"

It's a selfish thought; that's why it's called a demon. Yet in His goodness, God has started to make me at peace with this by reminding me that He was pleased with me then and remains pleased with me even now.

His grace is sufficient.

And that, perhaps, is exactly how He wants me to continue to experience *Cancer With Grace.*

The Doctor Wants to See Both of Us
by Barney Hilton Murray

Originally published in Good News Tucson in 2009

The doctor wants to see both of us.

My wife has cancer.

When my daughters were growing up, the last thing they wanted to hear from me was, "I need to see you in my office." Not that I had an office, but hearing that meant that,

1. They were in some form of trouble and
2. That the result would be a spanking, punishment, or even worse, a lecture.

So when my wife told me that the doctor wanted to see both of us, I knew this couldn't be good.

As we were hearing what the near future was going to be like for us and what the medical field had planned, with all the answers we were getting, not all of the questions were being addressed. With all of the natural questions regarding the treatment process and necessary lifestyle changes, the one big question that was answered almost immediately from within was "Why?" The answer, "That God might be glorified."

Now a lot of family and friends are going to be impacted by this, but what about the three main lives? Jacki, me and the life we have together. What about us? For God to get the glory out of this chapter in our lives, what do we have to do? We have never been here before. We have been through a lot together, but nothing like this. This is at a whole new level.

Once we embraced the fact that God was in control, and true, this is at a new level, everything we had gone though individually and collectively was in preparation for "such a time as this." In our spirits we believed that God was going to help us through the process and we would be left with a testimony and a greater trust in Him. This was not about Jacki nor I but more about the lives that her testimony was going to touch and restore hope for those in need.

As a husband and father, on the spiritual level I understood that I was also being tested and need to exercise faith and trust in God. On the natural level, I was challenged emotionally and intellectually.

Where was I going to get the strength to meet Jacki's needs, reassure her that I love her and meant it when I said "...in sickness and health." How was I going to be strong enough to hold the family together and let them see that what we tried to teach them about the power of God is no joke. Family far and near would see and hear the peace of God in our conversation and day-to-day interaction. How was I going to concentrate at work knowing my wife is suffering with a disease I can't even pronounce? I didn't know.

The one thing I did know was I didn't have a choice. If I was going to be successful in all I had to do, and be true to my commitment to my God, my wife and my family, I had to rely on God to get me through this and to be obedient to His directions.

I believe that a blessed life in Christ is possible when you forego your opinions and discussions and take heed to His word. I have found when you develop "blind obedience" to the Word of God, you are executing based on your faith and trust in Him and I believe God honors that.

I was interviewed by a fellow journalism student who was working on an article about older people returning to school. During the interview, family life came up and I shared what Jacki and I had gone through. She asked, "How did you do it?" She seemed to be in disbelief that we could have been through so much and still be together. "I know some men would have left and buckled under the pressure," she said. This may be true. When I told her I didn't have a choice and there was no decision to make about caring for my wife, she wanted to debate that you always have a choice. After much discussion, I could see that this was a concept that she just didn't get. The power of love and commitment when combined with Christ becomes one of the strongest forces known to man.

My wife is now two years cancer free. I am excited and relieved as well. As I look back over the process, there were so many things going on it all is somewhat of a blur to me. I tried to do what I thought I had to do to the best of my ability. Yes I was scared. Felt helpless at times. Wished it was me instead. Couldn't imagine what life would be like without my Jacki.

Thank God, I don't have to.

Philippians 4:13 (New International Version)
I can do everything through him who gives me strength.

Chapter Eight

"It's not about you, Jacki."

**A conversation with
the *Cancer With Grace* characters**

*From interviews with (in order of appearance) Aryn
Murray, Aja Williamson, Debra Lopez, Davita West-
brook, Andrea Kwakye, Sandra Barnes Pennington,
Elaine Walker, Della Stein, Carolynn Bonner, Clara
Jones, Germaine Romero, and Janice Charles. Written
by the editor.*

As a physiology and anatomy major, **Aryn Murray**, the youngest of Jacki's two daughters, certainly had a unique response when she found out that her mother had a rare form of head and neck cancer found primarily in Asian men who were smokers.

"I took on the role of trying to explain to my family what it was and break it down for them so they could understand it," she said. "I didn't get a chance to react because I felt the need to not only say what the cancer meant, but to try to communicate what was going to happen next." Aryn said this mental process helped her through the initial shock of the news—and prevented her from sinking into despair. "I was busy on the computer and I didn't talk much about it. I just started to work and kept my mind busy. I did it so I could talk to my mom and answer any questions," Aryn said, "but mostly it was for my dad. He had to take in all of the information and be a support for her. That way he could know what mom was going to need or anticipate what was going to come."

Aryn filled this vital role from her home in Phoenix while working and taking care of her young daughter Arilàn. Older daughter **Aja Williamson**, on the other hand, lived in Tucson, allowing her to take on a different role. "I made it a point to always be around, though to be honest I was mostly there for me," she said. "Mom's cancer never seemed to stand in the way of what was going on in our household. It was never mentioned to us just how sick she was. She was very adamant that things should go on as usual. It was never a question." Throughout the months of treatments and recovery, Aja visited Jacki almost every day, often with her little son Aren. "Mom was great to talk to and to hang out with; we had great conversations," she said, adding that she particularly enjoyed talking with Jacki about her pregnancy with her second child Alijah. "It was a relief to me to be able to talk to somebody about it, but I'm sure it was a relief to her, too, that we weren't talking about her cancer."

Aryn was also pregnant during the time Jacki was battling cancer, and it was an especially challenging time for her. Aryn was diagnosed at age nineteen with a chronic liver disease that creates a secondary disease when she's pregnant, dramatically increasing the chances of stillbirth by four-to-one in the final trimester. She had to constantly monitor her own health while dealing with her mother's cancer. "Because I've been sick since I was nineteen, I've learned how to adapt my life so people around me don't know that I'm sick. I worried about mom...(and) the more I worried, the more I felt like I had to step back from the cancer so that the stress of it didn't affect my pregnancy any worse than it already was. It was hard for me, too, because I wasn't there in Tucson. I felt bad about that."

Aryn gave birth to her son Ajani at 10:00 am on April 15—and just hours later received a call from Jacki to learn that her mom no longer had cancer. "It was one of those times where you cannot doubt that God exists," Aryn said, admitting that her faith wavered throughout her mother's cancer.

"It's one of the greatest days in my life."

"Then I get to the day that my son is born, he's alive, and then my mom calls and says she's cancer free. It's one of the greatest days in my life. I just felt the beauty and blessing of life."

Aryn said that day had another significant outcome. "It was a turning point in my need to better my relationship with my mom. We do not run in the same lane at all on anything. Growing up, I always kept a distance; therefore, I never really saw all the work she was doing and all the time she was putting in to make me who I was. I never felt the need to try to figure her out and connect with her. Now, I definitely know who she is and I understand a lot of why she does what she does, even if I'm still running in Lane A and she's still in Lane B. That's okay, because now our relationship is based on facts and not just perception. It's grown up."

Aja also looks back with appreciation at her mother's battle with cancer. "It's weird to say it; 'My mom had cancer.' Today nobody would ever know," she said. "I wouldn't have the relationship I have with her now if she hadn't gone through that and had I not been there with her. I'm not sure how I dealt with it, but we just kept on moving."

Among the others who kept on moving during Jacki's bout with cancer were the friends who prayed for her and stood with her throughout the ordeal—all of whom had been helped by Jacki in some way in the years prior to the diagnosis. **Debra Lopez** had brain aneurysms that nearly took her life back when Jacki helped comfort and support Debra's daughters during a month-long hospital stay. When she learned Jacki had cancer, she decided to commit to call Jacki every Saturday morning at 8:00 a.m.

"God told me that I needed to be supportive of her as she had been supportive of me when I almost died. He said, 'You need to show her the same love she did for you and your family," Debra said. "Some Saturdays she felt like talking; others she was too weak or not feeling well. I wasn't used to hearing her in a weak form. She was always a strong woman of God to me. But calling her helped me because I was going through an ugly divorce at the time and it gave me strength listening to her be so positive and upbeat and having so much faith. My divorce was nothing in comparison. I knew I'd be fine because Jacki said I was going to be fine."

Davita Westbrook first met Jacki when they sang together in the church choir in California, "bonding over silly jokes while trying not to get caught by the choir director," she said. "It was one of those moments when you just know you've found a person who will become important to you." Davita oversaw the singles ministry at the church while Jacki and Barney eventually directed the ministry to married couples. One day, Davita shared how Sunday was one of the most difficult days for single people because they had nowhere to go when couples and families went home together after service. Jacki and Barney invited Davita to come home with them, along with a number of other close friends from church, an offer that eventually led to the creation of "family dinner." "This was once or twice a month," Davita said, "a combination of singles and married couples who became each other's family. The kids called us 'uncle' and 'auntie.' We thought of each other as true brothers and sisters though none of us was blood-related. At these gatherings, we shared food, we celebrated birthdays and holidays, we played games, we discussed the Word, and we prayed over each other. It was the closest thing to how the early church must have been that any of us had ever experienced. It lasted for a year, maybe longer, before people started moving away." Davita left to return to Massachusetts before Jacki and Barney moved to Arizona. "Our little family was fractured," Davita said. "We cried and cried."

Davita and some other members of that church family were reunited, though, in the PIT Crew prayer team after Jacki's cancer diagnosis, and Davita was also felt led by God to dedicate extra time to contact Jacki, calling her twice daily during treatments. "When she first told me about the cancer," Davita said, "I could feel myself screaming on the inside. When I got off the phone, I cried like a baby. I felt in my heart of hearts that we might lose her. It was such a serious diagnosis. All I could think of was Barney and the girls without her. I was devastated."

She said praying for Jacki was a humbling experience. "Jacki is used to being the strong one for everyone else. For her to allow herself to be vulnerable and to share with us what she was going through was an honor to be considered a part of her inner circle," Davita said. "God brought to my remembrance to call and I prayed to have the right things to say at the right time. I wanted to hug her and hold her hand and take her to treatments, but I couldn't do those things. All we had were our voices on the phone. She heard in my voice how much I cared about her and worried over her. Sometimes she said, 'Today was a bad day,' and she didn't want to talk about it, but then you stay on the phone and hear each other breathe and you understand what is being said in the silence. The presence of that other person is precious and brings comfort."

Before her son was born, **Andrea Kwakye** was facing major surgery at the same time she was separated from her husband Charles. "My mom came out to help me, and I didn't know it then, but my mom told me Jacki went to the hospital and sat with her the whole time I was in surgery. It was the first time she'd met my mom. My mom was so grateful." Andrea recovered and gave birth to a son to whom Jacki and Barney ultimately became godparents. Jacki and Barney also served as Bible study leaders for Andrea and Charles. "We went through some tough patches in our marriage. They coached us through, and we're still together today after almost twenty years as husband and wife," Andrea said.

When Jacki was diagnosed with cancer, she needed expensive dental work to be completed before radiation treatments could begin. According to Andrea, "They were not in the financial situation at that time to take care of it. I'm a giver and I fundamentally believe God blesses you to be a blessing to others." Under God's direction, Andrea sent Jacki and Barney the amount needed to cover the need. "While it wasn't a small amount of money, in God's hand it was. God had given me a lot of favor, and through that favor I was able to give back."

During Jacki's cancer, Andrea said she gained a new appreciation for life. "Sometimes we take certain things or relationships for granted, and for me that was very critical. At that time, I was coming off my son having to go through a liver transplant. It was an emotional rollercoaster watching Jacki go through that, and having gone through what I went through, you just have to trust God for the very air that you breathe knowing that our time here, and our relationships here, are so important."

> *"You just have to trust God for the very air that you breathe."*

Sandra Barnes Pennington describes Jacki as being a "lifeline for me in a very difficult time in my marriage. I was looking for an accountability partner—and I had someone completely different in mind. When the Lord said it would be Jacki, I was really afraid. I thought, 'She's perfect. She's the diva.' That's what we called her. I'm so *not* a diva. I was completely intimidated." Then she heard Jacki speak at church one Sunday morning and immediately learned that the diva was far from perfect and had actually experienced many of the same challenges Sandra was then facing. "She was an amazing woman of God who, through a very challenging time, shared with me what I needed to hear from a biblical perspective as opposed to agreeing with me in my anger."

"She counseled me as a mentor for about three years. She was all up in my business," Sandra said. "So when she was diagnosed with cancer, my prayer to the Lord was, 'I don't know how I can help in this situation or how you want to use me, but I'm just available for you. Show me what to do.'"

God responded to Sandra's prayer one morning as she was reading a devotional from Our Daily Bread. "I was at work, and Jacki and I had just talked on the phone about some of the needs she had at that time," Sandra said. "The devotional talked about God being available to help a friend in need, and it concluded with the question, 'What would you do to help a friend?' God had provided some money and I have a spirit of giving. Suddenly, I knew exactly what to do." The result? Her distinctly diva-type letter to Jacki and Barney, dated April 2, with the "rules" on how to spend a $750 gift (see Chapter 4).

Four other PIT Crew members shared how they were impacted by God as they prayed for Jacki. **Elaine Walker** was led by God to pray for Jacki to be persistent in her faith. "The Lord revealed to me that as long as she stayed in or increased in her faith, she would be okay," Elaine said. "With that, my faith grew because I saw the promises of God manifest in her as she went through her ordeal, and He used that to help me and the whole PIT Crew to increase our faith. He was faithful, and it helped me understand that no matter what the enemy tries to do to us, God is greater."

Della Stein was helped by Jacki when her mother was battling multiple sclerosis. "My first reaction to Jacki's cancer was shock because at that time I had two other dear friends go through cancer and neither one survived. It was scary, but there was also this feeling that Jacki is kind of bigger than life, like a parent who is always strong." As part of the PIT Crew, Della remembers instances of "praying together on the phone and feeling a sense of strength that it was going to be okay. We encouraged each other about God's ability to heal and the power of believing."

Carolynn Bonner kept an archive of Jacki's random email reflections that were sent by Jacki to Carolynn throughout the period she fought cancer. "They ranged from a sentence to a paragraph. Some days I read them; other days I didn't. Yet even in the midst of all she was going through, her faith never wavered. It encouraged me. I was supposed to be her stronghold, but she was my stronghold."

Clara Jones saw her role on the PIT Crew as a sacred trust. "When I'm your friend, you'll always be in my heart. I give you my whole heart and not just a part of it," she said. "I felt like it was my duty to pray for Jacki because she's my sister in Christ. We weren't going to give up. We were going to do our duty until she was healed."

Germaine Romero, Jacki's surprise visitor for Thanksgiving, said she was inspired at how Jacki never acted like she was sick. "She's never been someone who is 'Woe is me.' God certainly used her for His glory. She is a living testament to what faith can do for you if you just believe," she said, adding that "we are to use our faith to help other people. Jacki's situation made my faith stronger because, when looking at what she's been through, I know faith is not wasted. I need faith to be able to put one foot in front of the other, especially when going through a crisis. No matter what I'm going through, I can just hold on and put it in God's hands."

111

For all of these special friends, they'll never forget their relief, joy, and unbridled praise to God when they learned Jacki was cancer free. Andrea was in New York state for the funeral of her best friend's mom when she received the news. "We know God is the healer and He's more powerful than anything we can go through," she said. "He chose to bring her through this for a purpose and for a reason; to be a blessing to others who may be going through what she's going through. His choice was that He needed this story to be told."

Sandra said she cried, danced, and worshipped God. "We knew it would be. It was awesome to watch how God delivered her in such a way that no man could take the credit." Elaine said she fell on her face before the Lord. "When she said she was cancer free, you can look back and see all that God was doing. Building her faith, building our faith—I saw a miracle happen! I asked God, 'I want to experience your miracle,' and I did through her experience."

Debra says the Lord used her participation in the PIT Crew to birth a personal prayer ministry. "As I prayed for Jacki," she said, "God taught me how to pray for other people. Now people call my house and ask for prayer, or if I can come and pray for them in person." She says she now has two "daughters"— girls from her church, one of whom has health problems and the other who has personal issues—that rely on her for prayer and even called her their "Mama D," a far cry from the lady who was once on death's door from the aneurysms.

"I'm still here because of the prayers of the righteous, so why not Jacki?" she asked. "I had an assurance about prayer. We believed God to heal her. God is a faithful God. It's what we prayed for. It's what we expected. It's what we got."

For Della, Jacki's healing from cancer affirmed that God's word is true. "We overcome by the blood of the lamb and the word of our testimony. It encourages me to know that God is the same. It's another building block that we can have faith for healing and for other areas of our life. God can deliver us. He cares for us." Clara adds: "He promises to give us the desire of our heart, and we wanted Jacki to be healed. There's no situation He can't handle."

Janice Charles, a self-proclaimed shopaholic, remembers sending Jacki a suitcase of clothes for her to wear during her weight loss from the chemotherapy treatments. "One of them was a pink suede coat, and breast cancer ribbons are pink, and that made me think about Jacki's heart. The breast is close to the heart, pink is close to the heart, and Jacki was close to my heart," Janice said. "She's a sister who, no matter what I was going through, was non-judgmental. She always told me what I sometimes didn't want to hear, but definitely needed to hear, from God through her. She's an encourager and a supporter." When Jacki was declared cancer free, she returned the pink coat to Janice. "When she sent it back," Janice said, "it was full circle."

The final word on Jacki and her healing comes from Janice and, as they say, it'll preach.

"God is a healer and He will show Himself to be a healer. Sometimes the devil got busy in my mind and said the cancer's gonna take her out. But God's promises are 'yes' and 'amen.' Thing is, we don't recognize the miracles that happen every day. We look at the biblical stories when God healed the lepers, make the lame to walk, and the blind to see, yet we don't even look at the small miracles that occur every minute that we live.

A breath is a miracle. A heartbeat is a miracle. Getting in your car and going from work to home is a miracle. There are still miracles that happen every day and in everything. If God is in all things and God is good, then nothing is bad. The focal point is the goodness of God."

"God's promises are 'yes' and 'amen.'"

"When we go before the Lord, we don't need to go before Him in a namby-pamby kind of way. We need to go before Him with intensity, because I feel the intensity of our prayers call for an immediate response. When you know that you know that you know, God is able to use anything that He creates to give Himself the glory."

About the Author

Jacquelyn D. Murray is a writer, speaker, singer, and teacher. She works in ministries to women and married couples at The Well Worship Center in Tucson, AZ under the leadership of Pastor Eli A. Lopez, and also serves as a member of the pastoral leadership team and the praise and worship team. Jacki is also a florist, enjoys reading, traveling, spending time with family and friends, and scrapbooking and other crafts. Jacki and her husband Barney celebrated 35 years of marriage in 2015 and have two adult daughters, Aja and Aryn, and seven grandchildren. Born in White Plains, New York, Jacki is the oldest of five children.

To request Jacki as a speaker, singer, or teacher, visit
www.jacquelyndmurray.com

Cancer With *Grace*

"Your Journey" Journal

Use each of these ten sections to write your responses and reflections on Jacki's questions, and to keep a prayer journal of your prayers to God on the topic—and His responses to you as a God of His word.

1. What is the most difficult situation you've gone through?

How did it affect you?

"Your Journey" Journal

"Your Journey" Journal

"Your Journey" Journal

2. Explain how your faith helped you during your hardship?

"Your Journey" Journal

"Your Journey" Journal

"Your Journey" Journal

3. Explain your relationship with God during your difficulty.

"Your Journey" Journal

"Your Journey" Journal

"Your Journey" Journal

4. Explain how your relationship with God changed after your hardship.

"Your Journey" Journal

"Your Journey" Journal

"Your Journey" Journal

5. How do you normally cope with trial?

"Your Journey" Journal

"Your Journey" Journal

6. Do have a "go to" person in your life that you can talk to about anything?

Describe that person.

"Your Journey" Journal

"Your Journey" Journal

"Your Journey" Journal

7. How do you cope with hardships when your "go to" person is unavailable?

"Your Journey" Journal

"Your Journey" Journal

"Your Journey" Journal

8. How do you respond to someone else's hardship?

"Your Journey" Journal

"Your Journey" Journal

"Your Journey" Journal

9. What part of **Cancer With Grace** touched you the most?

Why?

"Your Journey" Journal

"Your Journey" Journal

"Your Journey" Journal

10. Can you relate to the experience Shared in Cancer With Grace?

How?

....

....

....

....

....

....

....

....

....

....

....

....

....

....

....

....

....

....

"Your Journey" Journal

"Your Journey" Journal